Forest H. Belt's

Easi-Guide to CAMPING COMFORT

Photography by Forest H. Belt
and Bonnie C. Smith

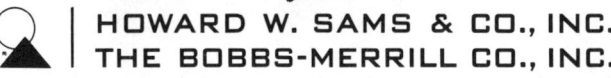

HOWARD W. SAMS & CO., INC.
THE BOBBS-MERRILL CO., INC.
INDIANAPOLIS · KANSAS CITY · NEW YORK

FIRST EDITION

FIRST PRINTING—1974

Copyright © 1974 by Howard W. Sams & Co., Inc., Indianapolis, Indiana 46268. Printed in the United States of America.

All rights reserved. Reproduction or use, without express permission, of editorial or pictorial content, in any manner, is prohibited. No patent liability is assumed with respect to the use of the information contained herein.

International Standard Book Number: 0-672-21128-9
Library of Congress Catalog Card Number: 74-81778

Preface

Our pioneer heritage in the United States has never entirely waned. Recently, in fact, it has manifested itself in a growing urge among Americans of all ages to head for the woods every summer weekend and holiday. Camping, once a pastime for Boy Scouts, hunters, prospectors, and fishermen, has captured the fancy of millions.

Camping today only vaguely resembles the outdoor living of Daniel Boone and Davy Crockett. The majority of modern campers converge on parks and campgrounds that offer facilities such as running water, flush toilets, and electricity. They drive rolling houses, called recreational vehicles. They in no way rough it like our pioneer forebears did. Yet they do find relaxation outside the city, in fresher air. And the whole notion of camping today generates an aura of comradeship that can only enrich each camper's experience.

Some campers bring tents to the campgrounds. Most of these, if they had their choice, would rather camp somewhere away from RV crowds. But truly primitive campsites are scarce. You can't just wander through any old woods and pitch camp where you please. Some farmer or timber-owner could evict you at gunpoint.

The tent camper, however, enjoys a closer communion with nature than RV drivers ever know exists. Truly rugged individuals head far into the wilderness, backpacking what they can carry and finding the rest of their living on the land. Even they encounter manmade restrictions as to where they can trek and what they can do there. But by and large, the tent camper and backpacker perceive glimpses of the true woodsman's life.

This book conducts you through a two-faceted realm of modern outdoor living. On the one hand you find the crafts and skills of the pioneer wilderness; on the other, the conveniences that impart a degree of comfort never dreamed of in frontier days. This amalgam of the old and the new spawns an approach to camping that offers the best of two worlds.

Many people today look on real outback camping as one long strenuous effort. That's why RVs are popular; they sport the labor-saver gadgets of home. Camping should not be a slave operation, and this book repeatedly shows how to stay out of that rut. Each chapter emphasizes quick and safe ways to accomplish camp chores, with an aim to leaving the most time for play or quiet rest.

The philosophy of camping propounded herein bears heavily on one central theme: *comfort*. Not lazy camping, but comfortable and relaxed camping. Dozens of photos enlarge your aptitude for spotting an easy campsite. Guidelines for situating your tent assure you maximum comfort from any surroundings. Furnishings bought or made embellish tent living. Chapters on keeping warm or dry or cool acclimate you for whatever weather you might encounter.

Mixing wilderness woodlore with campground convenience amasses a camping wisdom exceptionally suited to present-day individual or family camping by RV or tent. The final pages reiterate what any camping experience should impart—a feeling of wholesome, relaxing rejuvenation. To that spirit I've dedicated this book.

As usual with my *Forest H. Belt's Easi-Guide* books, many people joined in the effort to make this book outstandingly useful. Bonnie C. Smith photographed some of the campground scenes, and Natalie New and Deborah McPherson made prints in the photolab. For other help and cooperation, I especially thank Edwin Taylor Belt, Jr., Becky Clingerman, Mr. and Mrs. Jack P. Comer, Violet Gianakos, the Indiana Department of Commerce, the Indianapolis Department of Parks and Recreation, David Kaufmann, Cindy Miller, Scott Rink, and Aloma, Alissa, Jennifer, and Timothy Wignall. They and I wish you many days of camping in woodland comfort.

Forest H. Belt

Contents

CHAPTER 1
In Search of the Better Campsite 7
   Scenic views—Facing the early morning sun—Where the recreational action is—High ground—Trees or no trees?—Dealing with hillsides—Ponds and streams—Cabins—Wilderness areas

CHAPTER 2
Houses Away From Home: Tents 21
   Sizes, shapes, and types—Staking and guy ropes—Tent fabrics—Insect netting and windows—The ground cloth or tent floor—Repelling insects—Caring for the floor—Setting up—Taking down—Folding for travel

CHAPTER 3
Cushy Living Inside a Tent 37
   Think comfort—Cots and mattresses—Indulge in a table—Camp stools—Lawn furniture for camp comfort—Lights

CHAPTER 4
Make Your Own Shelter 45
   Poncho for wilderness protection—Tarpaulin as all-purpose shelter—Lean-to and crackerbox—Pup tent from tarp—Cave and overhang shelters; dangers—Old farm buildings—Lean-to from tree branches

CHAPTER 5
Keeping Dry 55
   Dampness your serious camp enemy—Reading the coming weather—Coping with rainstorms—Tents in rain—Preparing for heavy winds—Importance of airing clothes and bedding—Footwear treatment—Rainwear

CHAPTER 6
Staying C-o-o-o-l 67
   Your body's air conditioning—Food and drink for hot days—Utilizing every breeze—Shade you find or build—Wet cloth coolers—Clothes for hot weather—Hats—Sunstroke and heat prostration—Swimming

CHAPTER 7
Ways to Stay Warm 79
   Prevent moisture accumulation—Keep off the ground—Winter clothing in layers—Coverings for extremities—Frostbite—Value of exercise—Using sunshine—Windbreaks natural and man-made—Heaters

CHAPTER 8
Campfires: The Camp Workhorse 99
> Small and efficient fires—Wood: kindling and burning fuel—Clean a fireproof circle—Reflectors—Cook over hot coals—Trench cookfire and how to build it—The star campfire—Smudge fires battle mosquitoes—Grills and camp stoves—Charcoal fires—The final touch: Quenching

CHAPTER 9
Safe, Tasty Eating and Drinking 117
> Examples of foods to carry camping—Beverages and desserts—Ice chests—Boiling and purifying water—Keeping food from animals

CHAPTER 10
Backpack Hiking in Comfort 133
> What to take along—How to pack it—Provisions for a wilderness trek—Emergency supplies—The pack and frame—Resting, day or night

CHAPTER 11
Relax or Run Ragged? 141
> Let no one be a slave—Everyone pitches in—Cook's day off—The way to live

Chapter 1

In Search of the Better Campsite

For anyone who knows how to camp, the mention of a woodland holiday stimulates visions of unabashed fun. It promises pleasure for adults and ecstasy for youngsters. Imagine—free in the wide outdoors!

But it's not that way for everyone. Camping imposes strains on some families that cancel all the joy. The reason simmers down to one factor: they aren't comfortable in camp. If you had to characterize camping pleasure in one word, the word would probably be *comfort*.

This book deals with the whole of camping. And this first chapter takes up the portion experienced campers recognize as paramount—the choice of a cozy campsite. You can train your eye to pick out a camp location that offers an inherent degree of comfort. You can also develop a knack for arranging your camp so you and your family are all comfortable. That assures the success of your outing.

Some of the thrill of camping derives from a love of nature. Fresh air smells sweet. You can exult in the sounds of birds and insects. Most outdoors lovers find their greatest pleasure in what they see.

Accordingly, choose campsites with the kind of view you like. Maybe it's meadows. Perhaps you prefer dark virginal woods. A panoramic view toward mountains may stir your fancy. Or maybe you want on top of a hill, to look out across the wide valley.

Reasons for choosing a scenic campsite are largely psychological. Imagine this incongruity: You walk out of your tent on a bright, sunny morning, with birds singing and a light breeze sifting through the trees—and across the way sits a junkyard or garbage dump. Ruins your illusion.

So much "civilization" has overspread the country, campsites with a pleasant view may seem scarce or nonexistent. Nevertheless, beautiful camping sites do exist, both in and out of national and state parks. Consider rural areas where you find scenery you like. You won't find yourself very welcome as a camper in most farm locales. Yet, do a little talking in places you're attracted to. Serious and conscientious campers eventually discover marvelous "unknown" areas open to them, far off the beaten track. Once you've unlocked that possibility, you can seek out a campsite that holds a view you enjoy.

Even when you enter a state or national campground, don't jump into the first spot you find vacant. Wander a little. Better yet, arrive a day ahead of the holiday or weekend rush and crowd. Select carefully the spot you set up camp. Start your effort toward camping comfort by finding a view that turns you on.

While you're hunting that perfect view, consider its direction. The front of your tent should face south or east. There are several reasons. The main one involves exposing your tent to the morning sun. A lot of dampness develops from the overnight dew. The bright sun of early morning goes a long way toward dispelling that dampness from the major "living" area in front of your tent.

Ideally, then, you want a southeastern exposure facing something scenic. That may sound finicky and to a degree it is. However, remember that camping comfort is your goal. A little extra looking around doesn't seem like too steep a price to pay.

If you must face your camp any direction other than southeast, try east or south. It's that forenoon sun you're after for the front of your tent.

Some of the pleasure in camping relates to your outdoor activity preference. If all you're after is a place to relax and read, or to browse nearby soaking up the outdoors, auxiliary activities don't matter too much. However, they're a part of camping for most people.

Water holds probably the greatest attraction—the playing kind of water. You may want to swim, boat, or water-ski. Or water may simply frame the kind of scenery you like best. Moonlight or sunlight rippling on a lake can certainly stimulate your visual sense.

If you want a popular and relaxing outdoor pastime, try fishing. You're forced naturally to set up camp near some body of water or stream. Still, keep in mind the criteria already discussed. Hold out for the view you want, and face your camp east, south, or southeast. You may as well hunt the best while you're looking.

Truly rustic camping leads you to bicycling or hiking trails. You can bicycle places you can't take a car. But you still keep to some sort of beaten path. Of course, some backwoods traces are too rugged for a cyclist. Along those trails you walk or pack with a horse. Hiking, you can literally go anywhere you want, on or off the trail. (You'll find more about bicycle camping in *Forest H. Belt's Easi-Guide to Multispeed Bicycles*.)

The upshot is this: Figure out what you like to do most and then select a camping area where you can. You are not obliged to make camping your sole—or even prime—reason for being there. Camping very often is a pleasant, low-cost way to overnight. Whether for horsebacking, cycling, skiing, or just plain woodcrafting, put your camp where your idea of action is.

Consider these precautions: Set up camp on high ground, if you can at all. That doesn't necessarily mean you have to be on a hill. But situate your tent and your camping activities in some spot that rain won't turn into a quagmire.

Water tends to collect in low areas. Even the most seemingly flat locations have depressions and small hillocks or mounds. If that's the best you have, pick a mound for your tent. You'll be glad, if rain happens along. At all costs, avoid sinks and swamps.

The neophyte camper seeks out trees. That's a good idea only if you approach the notion correctly. You do want trees for shade, particularly in the afternoon. But pitching your tent under trees invites two problems. In heavy winds, dead tree limbs fall around you. A large one could cause injury or damage. Just as annoying, trees drip for hours after a rain. Your tent takes hours or even a day or two to dry out if leaves are dribbling water on it.

The ideal setup has your tent facing a bit east of south with trees standing several yards away toward south and west. That brings you sunshine in the morning when you and your tent need the warming up and drying out. Later in the day, say from noon on, the temperature climbs and you need the shade. The sun has moved around, and trees situated to the southwest and west place your camp in shade all afternoon and evening.

Obviously, these are ideal situations. Yet, once you become accustomed to examining these qualities in a campsite, you'll be astonished how often you can find almost exactly what you want. It merely takes getting there ahead of the crowd and doing a little shopping around.

13

Camping on a hillside gives you drainage in case of rain, but sleeping can be downright uncomfortable. You can't always find a level spot. If you camp much in parks, you know how crowded they are most of the time. A late arrival finds the level ones almost invariably taken.

Faced with hillside camping, you have several courses to choose from. In the wilds, you can scoop out a flat place for your tent. That lets you set it up level. In parks you can't do that. If your tent has no bottom in it, you could scoop out places for sleeping before you put down your ground cloth. If you sleep on camp cots, turn them crosswise of the grade and raise the downhill legs on flat stones or even pieces of wood. Sleeping in bags, you can lie crosswise of the hill; roll a blanket lengthwise, and prop your sleeping bag on the downhill side.

Similar ingenuity can solve most problems of camping on a steep hillside. Nevertheless, the best solution lies in avoidance. Accept a hillside campsite only as a last resort.

You'll encounter other difficulties from time to time. The countryside you choose for camping may be rocky. You'll find not only large rocks but small, sharp jagged rocks. Small stones strewn around the area bring two problems. In the first place, they're doggone uncomfortable to sleep on. Second, they quickly ruin the bottom of a tent or your ground cloth.

A rocky campsite leaves you no alternative but to pick up rocks before you put down your tent or sleeping bag. Actually, in all but the most rock-free spots, you'll want to sweep any tent site clean with your camp broom or a brushy limb before you set up. This contributes to comfort as well as adding life to your camp goods.

Consider safety before you pitch a tent, too. Look up as well as down. Look all around for dead tree limbs hanging and rotten snags standing. These are the first to come down in a heavy wind. Make sure your tent and campsite are far enough away to miss the crushing blow. When you have doubts, push such deadfalls down. They make a good source of firewood, incidentally, where using them is not forbidden.

Camping near a pond, you may feel like a latter-day Thoreau at Walden. But know the disadvantages. You can't use the water for drinking, without extensive treatment. Mosquitoes and snakes proliferate around the soggy edges and marshy grasses of ponds.

But camping by a pond isn't all bad. There might be small fish to catch and throw back. Some ponds have fish large enough to eat. The chug of bullfrogs at night can be fascinating sleep tonic. If you're quiet and unobtrusive, you stand high chances of observing wildlife come to drink.

You may prefer a stream. Along very fast brooks, you can worry less about water snakes such as the poisonous moccasin. Where the water deepens into quiet pools, the risk rises. Even so, camping along a stream has attractions. Some of the pools hold fish. Rock collectors find a wealth of specimens. The water is less likely to be contaminated, particularly when it runs fast over rock shallows. Yet, never drink it without treating it (pages 130–131).

Be cautious swimming in a pond or stream. Ponds hold two dangers: pollution and mire bottoms. You can encounter serious trouble swimming in a pond. The pollution factor affects streams too. You never know what was poured in a few miles upstream. Large rivers can be dangerous for both pollution and tricky currents. Swim in regular facilities if possible, and NEVER swim alone.

You don't have to tent-camp to enjoy outdoor living. A cabin doesn't really put you outdoors, but it can offer a rustic way to live. You can expect more comfort than in a tent. Built-in bunks might make sleeping easier. You can have mattresses, or straw. For wintertime camping, a cozy cabin may seem not much apart from living at home. Even without kitchen or bathroom facilities, or showers or air conditioning, a well designed cabin beats a tent (usually).

If you're building a cabin for summer (or winter) vacations, observe the same criteria you would for planning a tent site. A southeast exposure puts morning sun at the front door. Arrange, if you can, so shade falls on the front door or porch from early afternoon on. Clear out dead limbs and trees. Consider the fire hazards around a cabin. Clean out underbrush that might carry a fire up to the cabin walls. In the autumn, rake up fallen leaves conscientiously; they are dangerous carriers of flame, even from a small fire.

The disadvantage of a cabin? You don't have choice of location, once the cabin is built. You can't discover new areas. Although . . . you might derive unexpected rewards exploring your own area thoroughly.

Often, the topmost attraction of camping is isolation. Homes and businesses so consistently pack us into tight proximity, aloneness suggests a distinctly relaxing change.

You don't find solitude these days in state or national parks—unless you can go during the week rather than on weekends. Then, search out the remote sections. You can't always camp just anywhere you wish, but park authorities will help you find the sort of camping you really want if you take the trouble to ask. Wilderness trails offer remoteness. Write the National Park Service, Washington, DC 20240, and ask for details of wilderness areas for backpacking and tent camping. Some are accessible by automobile; others you have to pack into by foot, horse, or perhaps bicycle.

As mentioned earlier, if you'll expend some time and effort, you might discover privately owned remote areas where you can camp. This is the most difficult sort of campsite to find, but you are assured of privacy once you locate such a spot. Also be assured that, if you mess it up, you'll never be welcome back. Camping on private land demands a far better knowledge of woodcraft and a far more considerate approach than camping in state parks where you can throw your garbage in trash barrels. If you want true isolation and privacy, you might have to work some for it.

But . . . if lots of company and new friends are your style, state and national parks are right down your alley. Summer weekends find campgrounds so crowded, you'll have all the neighbors and company you can use. They offer great opportunities to befriend people whose interests are similar to yours. Many lasting friendships are formed over a neighborly campfire.

If you mix your camping with travel, and are simply overnighting along the way, you'll meet a new group of people every night. Camping out has become almost a way of summer life for some families.

There also is a happy medium. You can have some semblance of privacy if you want it. Simply pick a camping area that has marked-out camping sites. Most campers respect the privacy you want. If noisy youngsters bother you, find a site away from central lights. In the evening, that's where they congregate. Or, watch for campgrounds that cater exclusively to tent campers. Recreational vehicles tend to carry families.

String up some ropes and hang blankets on them if you want a little more privacy. Take advantage of natural barriers such as shrubbery.

Chapter 2

Houses Away
From Home: Tents

As much as any other factor, family size determines the tent for you. Of course there are other considerations. Something small, inexpensive, and simple suffices for mere shelter while you sleep. But for head room, or separate privacy inside the tent, you can buy large sizes complete with rooms.

Go to a camping store and look at what's available. The sporting goods departments of national chain stores stock tents in a variety of sizes, shapes, and prices. Study the summer catalogs mailed out by some of these concerns. In tuck-ins with your Sunday newspaper, you'll find camping gear on sale all through the season. Toward autumn, you'll find bargains in some of these flyers.

The photos in this chapter illustrate popular tent styles. You'll see tent materials, and how to care for them. You can make your tent truly a comfortable way to live outdoors.

The *umbrella* tent has been a long-time favorite. It's fine for a small family, with maybe one child. Part of its popularity stems from its low cost. It's easy to set up, and generally includes ground cloth and a small canopy in front of the door. The better versions include mosquito-netting windows and storm flaps. Some have a triple door: a zipper door of mosquito netting; an outside zippered door of canvas, in case of rain; and the canopy, which you can lower for a storm windbreak.

The smaller *mountain* tent accommodates only two people. But it's great for backpackers and people who travel into the deep wilderness. It's light to carry, quick to set up, and provides dependable shelter for two people. The better ones nowadays are of nylon, but you can still buy duck or drill versions. The ground cloth forms an integral part of the tent.

The *pyramid,* a teepee-type tent, has many advantages of the mountain tent. It's lightweight, particularly in its nylon version, and folds down into a small packet. Complete with jointed aluminum center pole, the whole thing weighs only two or three pounds. If you're headed into forested areas, with limbs overhead, you can stake out the bottom and support the top over a limb with a rope. This tent gives two people lots of room, and four can squeeze in. Two or three sleeping bags are no problem at all. The tent is all one piece—that is, the floor is sewn in. You needn't even dig trenches to keep water out.

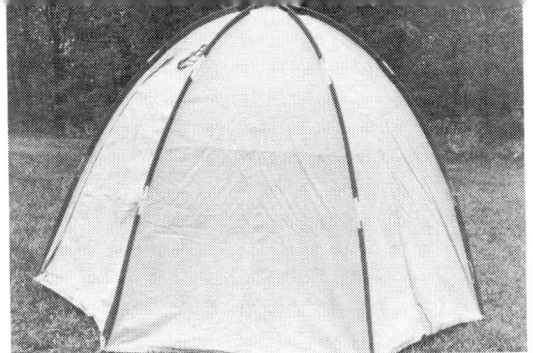

One simple tent is the *popup*. It has an external rib structure and you simply snap each support member into position. This tent is quick and easy to set up or take down and isn't inconvenient to transport. It holds two people comfortably.

The *cabin* tent, at the center, has become the popular tent for modern camping families. A small 8 × 10-foot size can accommodate four people comfortably and six if you arrange carefully. It's not too expensive, and is rather easy to travel with.

A self-supporting framework of three support bars is one of its major advantages. Aluminum rods join into a U-shaped center support and two eave-bars. Pages 32–33 lend some idea of how easily a tent like this goes up. With the bottom properly staked down, the angular structure of the frame provides sturdy support even in heavy winds.

Large families who do a lot of camping buy multiroom family tents. A *patio* tent has a room of netting plus a fully enclosed room for privacy. You can dine or loaf in the screened "patio" where evening breezes reach you but mosquitoes or flies don't. Such tents come in various sizes and can cost several hundred dollars.

Today's aluminum frames are staunchly self-supporting. But large tents have so much canvas area, it's a good idea to tie down with stakes and guy ropes.

23

There's a knack to staking out and securing a tent properly. When you drive stakes to hold the floor flat, point the sharp ends toward the center of the tent. The reason for this becomes obvious once you raise the tent. If you drive them outward, the slant lets the tent pull them straight out of the ground. If you drive them correctly, the pull of the tent is at right angles. The stake can't pull out without tearing up the ground. Stretch the floor smooth before you stake it.

Shopping for tent stakes nowadays, you have a choice between high-impact plastic and metal stakes. Plastic stakes last longer. You can't bend them, they don't rust, and they really are quite tough to break. It's possible to break off the little hook that keeps the tent guy rope from sliding up and off. Be careful if you pry your stakes out of the ground with the handaxe, as most seasoned campers do.

If you use guy ropes with your stakes, buy sliders to adjust the rope lengths. You can use the sheepshank knot, but the little metal sliders certainly save a lot in time and effort, particularly if you need to tighten or loosen guys in a hurry. Sisal or hemp rope stretches and shrinks with humidity. Nylon rope doesn't. You'll have to use guy ropes with a dining fly or awning (page 71).

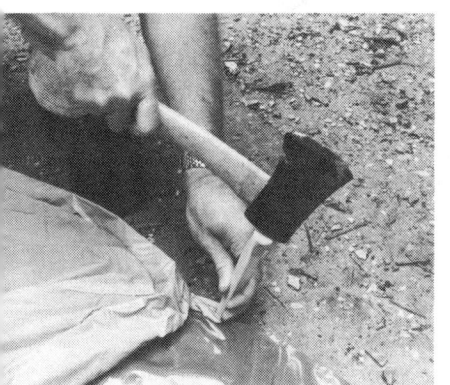
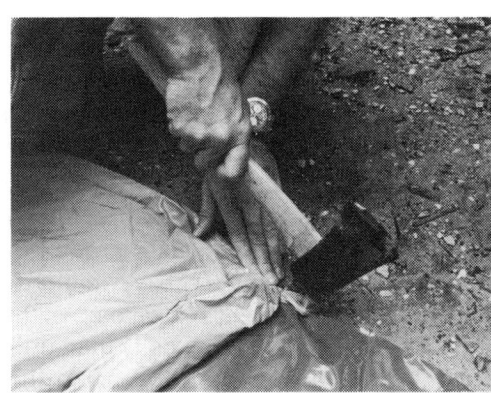

25

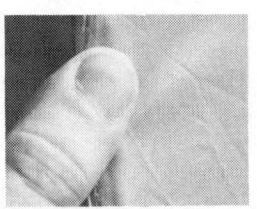

The material in the tent you buy is important. Nowadays, there are three major fabrics. Most common and least costly is drill, a lightweight form of canvas. Quality usually goes by the weight of a square yard. A 7-oz drill has the strength needed for a tent. You can identify drill by the diagonal shape of its weave. Duck is a heavier grade of canvas, with a square weave. It's used mainly in heavyweight tents intended for long bivouacs in the wilderness. It takes 8-oz or 10-oz duck to make a good tent. It's much more costly than drill.

Newly popular is nylon. It is not a new material, but older varieties didn't "breathe" well enough in tents to suit most campers. Lately nylon has been working out quite well for those who use it. It isn't as subject to mildew and other problems casual campers have with duck and drill. It's water repellant and very light to transport. A large tent folds down into a compact parcel. The better nylon tents have vinyl-impregnated (called Vinylon) roof and floor.

You should concern yourself with flammability of the tent you buy. Some duck and drill have been treated to make them fire retardant. No tent is fireproof. If you hold the cloth in a flame, it burns. However, some older tent fabrics are intensely flammable. If the flame from your campfire happened to trail some dry ground cover to your tent edges—poof! Don't buy any tent not guaranteed nonflammable. Nylon doesn't really burn. It melts. A spark lighting on it won't ignite the material, but flames nearby can damage it severely.

Before you buy a tent, study the insect netting that covers doors and windows. The netting should be woven fine enough to prevent all but the very tiniest of gnats from slipping through. Then, you can spray it with bug repellant to keep out even those little fellows. If you accidentally poke the netting with a stick, its weave shouldn't open up and leave a hole. Certainly, if it does, you should be able to work the threads back together to close the hole naturally.

You'll want insect netting over windows, because you need light and ventilation inside the tent. Some people feel claustrophobic shut up in a tent with no means of seeing out. Nylon tents let in a lot of light on their own, when the sun shines on them. Duck and drill don't allow much light through.

Netting at the door should be heavy enough that running the zipper up and down doesn't fray it.

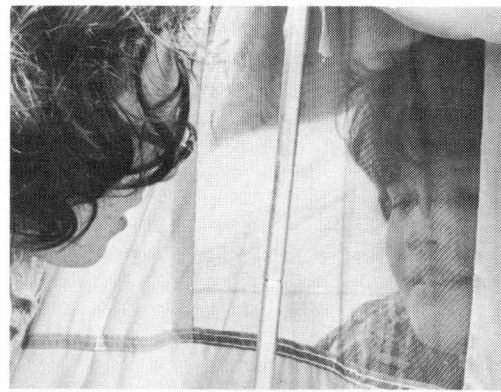

Check the door and window closures on any tent you plan to buy. Never buy a tent in a box without having seen a similar model set up. Photographs in catalogs and drawings on boxes are not always accurate. You should know whether the tent has windows on two sides or three. If you want to see out a lot, three windows are important. Insist on screen netting over the main door or at least in part of it. The netting should be coverable by a flap or "door" of weatherproof material so rain can't blow in.

Check how easily and quickly you can close the window flaps in case of storm. In some modern tents, with nylon netting, closures are on the inside. They simply zip up. Rain doesn't hurt the netting. Cotton netting deteriorates if it gets wet very often. Rainflaps on the outside, you roll up and tie in nice weather, and you roll down and tie for inclement weather or at night.

Your tent should close tightly at the bottom, even with a fairly high "sill." You want it to shut out crawling insects. Some have zippers, some have snaps. Obviously the zippers close more completely. Least desirable are tie-type closures.

If you have zipper closures, learn to take care of them. Never let loose threads accumulate in the zipper teeth. If a zipper track breaks at one point, try sewing the cloth tightly right next to the two teeth where the zipper has broken. Sometimes that'll hold the teeth close enough together that you can run the zipper across the break. It might last until you can have a new zipper put in.

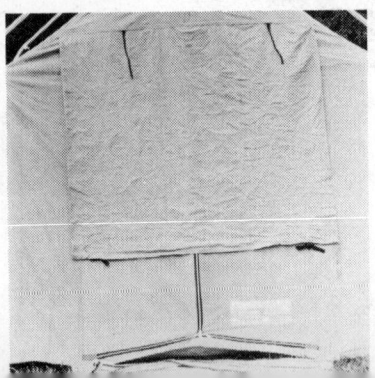 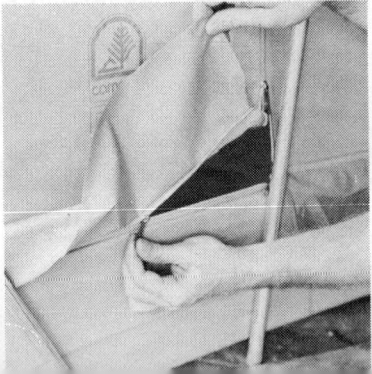

A tent with a ground cloth sewn in, and windows of a good quality netting, averts trouble with insects, particularly the flying kind. Tents with the ground cloth seam well above ground level keep out most crawling insects. However, spiders don't mind crawling over a high threshold. Buy an insect spray to take care of these for you. Ask for the kind that eliminates spiders, ants, and other crawling insects on contact.

Spray all around the tent openings. At the door, don't just spray at the threshold. Encircle the door perimeter with the repellant. As extra precaution, spray all the way around the floor or ground cloth seam. If the seam is at the ground, spray both dirt and tent freely. If you ditch the tent, do your spraying afterward. Spray immediately after a heavy rain.

Most insects and spiders are harmless. But some are not, and it's those you want to get rid of. Not many campers like little bugs of any sort crawling around inside the tent. A good spray also helps keep ticks away. They have an uncanny knack for finding wherever people are. And certain ticks, as you may know, are very dangerous.

Obviously, a sewn-in ground cloth works better than one just spread on the ground. Shop around a little, and you'll find tents with the ground cloth or floor seam a few inches above ground level. This offers advantages and disadvantages.

On the good side, it deters creeping or crawling animals such as snakes and lizards. They almost never crawl over a threshold like this. Among the disadvantages of the raised-seam tent floor, you'll find accumulated dirt more difficult to sweep out than in a tent whose seam is right at ground level. You have to sweep everything over near the door and use a piece of newspaper or cardboard as a dustpan.

The tent floor must not "breathe," for that allows moisture to accumulate inside when there's a heavy rain. The tent floor must be completely waterproof, probably nowadays a material impregnated with vinyl plastic. The thinness of some tent floor material makes it more susceptible to wear and rips. You have to exercise particular care with it.

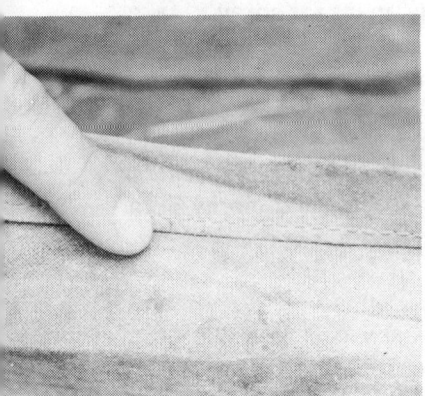

Rocks, sticks, and bits of debris can devastate the floor of a tent. As you walk inside, even with bare feet, the pressure brings on punctures and tears. A puncture in the tent floor lets in moisture and insects. The preventive is to sweep the area thoroughly and carefully before you put the tent down. Leaving your shoes outside the door helps. If you insist on wearing shoes inside the tent, which contributes to the dirt problem, make sure they are soft-soled gym shoes or moccasins.

Also sweep off the tent bottom when you break camp (page 35).

Keep dirt, rocks, and pebbles swept up and thrown out as they accumulate inside the tent. Don't set sharp table legs directly on the tent floor. Make some 6 × 6-inch plywood coasters that spread the weight of table legs over large areas rather than in four tiny spots.

One more caution relating to the floor of your tent. Never let moisture accumulate underneath. Be sure the tent site is adequately drained, as described on page 58. If moisture gets underneath, strike the tent and dry the bottom out.

Some campers put down a waterproof ground cloth beneath the tent floor. This is excellent when you expect to leave the tent up more than just two or three days. Even so, sweep the area underneath clean of junk. If you don't carry a broom, sweep with brushy tree limbs. Pick up all rocks and sticks. This little extra effort does more than merely make your stay more comfortable. It helps your tent floor last years longer.

Your tent came with instructions for setting it up. To supplement them, here are some hints that make tent living a bit easier.

Pull the floor taut when you stake it out. Follow the staking suggestions on page 25, so the tent stays firmly anchored.

The center U-shaped support (self-supporting frame) goes up first. Assemble the horizontal bar and thread it into the peak loops. Insert the vertical rod or poles at each end, and then ascertain that the end straps (center photo) have been pulled firm. Otherwise the peak of the tent won't stay smooth for best water repellancy.

Assemble the horizontal bars of both eave supports next, and string them through the eave loops. Again tighten the web straps at the curved ends. Then point the downturns *toward the center pole* and insert the poles that support the eave bars. The support poles slant upward from the center of the tent to the eaves. Position them, and then slide the bottom tips outward. This lifts the eaves into tight position.

Walk around the tent and even up all the poles. The tent should be firm but not stretched tight. Leave enough slack that the tent seams don't take a lot of strain. The "truss" shape of the frame and tent prevents blowing away.

When it comes time to take the tent down, make sure it's dry all over. If you roll your tent up with moisture trapped inside, you issue an invitation to mildew and rot. In hot, damp climates, a badly packed tent can rot in less than a month.

The best way to dry a tent is to let the sun shine on it. If it's in the shade, move it. If you have to, strike it and drape it across your car or a rope line where the sun can reach it. When you're merely overnighting, breaking camp early in the morning creates a problem. Vinyl-coated and nylon cloth doesn't rot like duck or drill does. Nevertheless, mildew can generate odors if you don't treat it as soon as you can.

If mildew does form, wash it off with a solution of 1 lb of bicarbonate of soda (baking soda) dissolved in a gallon of water. Scrub the mildew area briskly with this solution. Then hang the tent so the spots get plenty of sunshine. The baking soda counteracts the detrimental action of mildew on the cloth. Sunshine helps kill the mildew fungus itself.

To reiterate, though, get the tent dry before you fold it for storage and you won't incur this problem in the first place.

A small bit of extra care when you take your tent down goes a long way toward making it easier to set back up. Better yet, taking the tent down properly and folding it right for storage and transport increases its life considerably.

First look the tent over. Use a whisk broom to brush off mud or trash that has accumulated on any outside surfaces. Remove the tent supports, but leave the ground cloth or floor stakes in the ground. They keep the floor taut until you've done the preliminary folding.

Arrange the tent top and sides neatly in a fairly square form. Naturally there will be folds; but make as few of them as possible and make them neat and straight. Smooth out wrinkles. This eliminates sharp creases in the final folding. Creases wear rapidly during transportation and storage.

Once you have it all smoothed out, fold the tent in one-thirds or one-fourths, depending on what length your carrying bag is. Fold one edge over to the center (for fourths).

Before you go any further, sweep off the exposed underside. Dirt and tiny gravel gnaw holes in the floor while the tent is rolled up and traveling.

Make the second fold from the other edge. Again, sweep off the exposed bottom. Fold the quarters together, and sweep again. Finally, as you roll the tent, sweep off the rest. This procedure adds years of life to your tent floor.

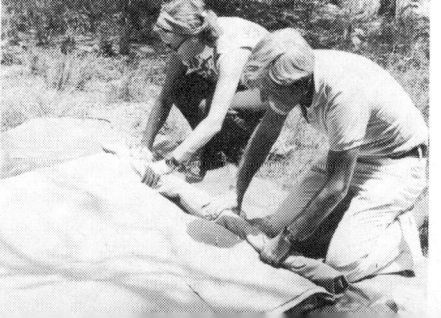

You can learn to erect most tents in 20–30 minutes and take them down in less. With cooperation from everybody in the family, you can cut camp chore time to a minimal portion of your camp day. Divide the work this way.

Dad unpacks the tent and drops it on the tent site. Older son sets the tent up. Dad meanwhile gets out food for the evening meal and camp furniture. Younger son or daughter gathers kindling for the fire. Mother pulls in slightly larger wood. And so on throughout the evening, everyone doing a share.

Following a routine like this, you can have camp pitched, supper done, and the evening campfire laid (but not yet lit) within an hour after picking your campsite and stopping. If you stop in late afternoon, that leaves time for swimming, tennis, hiking, bike riding, horsebacking, exploring, or whatever. Or . . . just prop your feet up and relax with a good book before dark. Your tent life should give you no more trouble than an evening at home. Plan it right and it can even be less work.

Chapter 3

Cushy Living Inside a Tent

Just because you leave your well-equipped house behind, that's no reason to forego comfort. The good life is not all a matter of running water and air conditioning. This chapter suggests some conveniences you can bring along to civilize your woods living.

Start by thinking in terms of comfort. Consider what all you want to do while you're out camping. Then equip your tent accordingly. Don't just run out and buy every piece of camp furniture you come across. Plan first. Think about it. Make a list. Do your shopping a little at a time, and late in the season. You find bargains in the fall, when stores are trying to clear out summer stocks.

Make your tent into a home away from home.

If you like to rough it, put your blankets or sleeping bag right on the tent floor. Of course, before the night is finished, your body feels every rock, stub, twig, and bump. Too, if the floor of the tent is vinyl, body perspiration dampens your bedclothes underneath you, and that spells discomfort.

Try a folding cot. Aluminum cots are lighter than wood, but the latter fold into a more compact package for traveling. You can stack some aluminum types into bunks, saving floor area while sleeping more people.

For comfort pick a cot that opens out flat—rather than one with undulations. A few campers try to use a chaise longue as a cot, making it do double duty. The type that folds out flat can support you comfortably at night, if it stays flat.

The cot material should be cloth. Plastic causes perspiration dampness even worse than you'll experience on the tent floor. The trouble is, plastic doesn't let air circulate next to your skin. Even a layer or two of blankets doesn't really help. The answer is a mattress that allows your body air.

So . . . when you buy a cot, consider (1) the space it takes up when you're traveling, (2) the space it occupies inside the tent, and (3) how much true comfort you can expect sleeping on it.

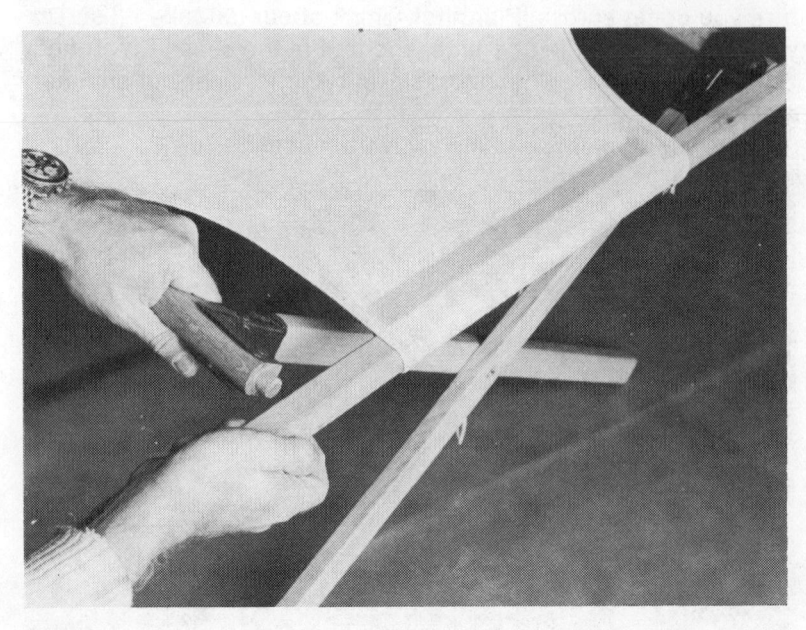

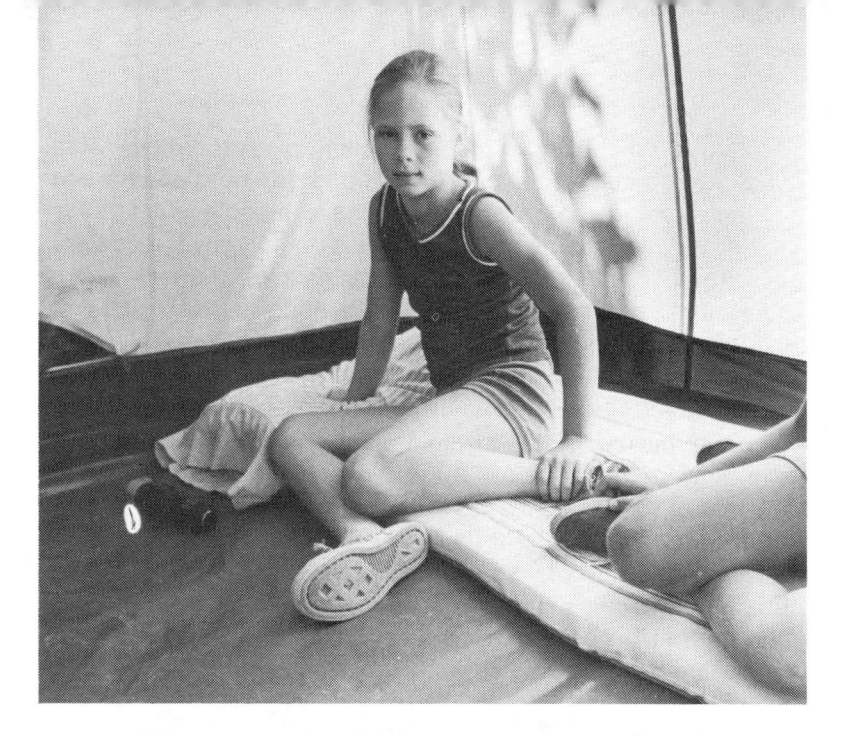

A mattress or pad on the tent floor can be comfortable. If it's a good mat, with good firm stuffing, it prevents bumps and pebbles from contributing to an aching back.

After the batting inside, the main consideration is what material you lie next to. Of course you'll put down blankets and/or your sleeping bag; but you still don't want to sleep next to leather or plastic. The reason has already been cited: the sweating problem. A few nights next to plastic causes your blankets or bag to absorb so much moisture you can't get a comfortable night's sleep. You may not even identify what keeps you awake, but it's the humidity of your bedclothes. Thorough airing every day helps, but it can't lick this problem. Bedclothes eventually build up such dampness and odor that you hate to use them.

That's why air mattresses are unsatisfactory for camping. They hide the lumps and bumps, but their waterproofing makes them poor for sleeping on.

Insist on a mattress with cloth on at least one side. If the mattress has some sort of cloth filling, such as Dacron, so much the better. Even foam under the cloth makes some people perspire in their sleep.

A couple of lightweight folding tables come in handy inside your tent. Without them, you do a lot of stooping, bending and kneeling. Most campers arrange to have a table outside the tent, but few put one inside. Yet, if comfort and convenience are your criteria, a small table with a shelf adds a lot.

You can use a card table, although that's more difficult to transport. A folding card table fits flat on the bottom of a small trailer, taking up almost no apparent space. In a car, hauling the same table would be virtually impossible.

You can make a "table" from a couple of wooden boxes and some plywood. Several 2 × 3-foot sheets of 1/4-inch plywood hold enough to make carrying them worthwhile.

Consider buying legs of the screw-in variety. You fasten the holders to one side of your pieces of plywood. The legs occupy little space traveling because you unscrew them from the plywood board. At camp, screw the legs on and you have instant tables. Two or three sets of these make a useful investment.

Roughing it, you sit on the floor of your tent. Outdoors you find logs or stumps to sit on.

But around the comfortable camp you'll find at least some small folding camp stools. They're handy, and little trouble to transport. Buy the kind with cloth seats. Whether you choose wooden or aluminum frames depends on preference. Aluminum is lighter, but wood seems more durable.

Camp stools are not for relaxing. They're for utility. When you have a chore you can sit and do, use a camp stool.

Preparations for cooking, camp equipment mending, and other chores go well from a camp stool.

For true relaxation, though, carry along something a little more comfortable.

Ordinary folding lawn furniture suits relaxation in camp. It's fairly lightweight to transport. It's durable year after year, providing you take care of it (mainly keep it out of the rain and weather when you're not using it). A chaise longue lets you stretch out. A rocker relaxes many people. The problem of lawn furniture, generally, is size. It's too bulky to stuff into a car trunk.

Regular folding camp furniture might be a better bet. For example, the "director's chair" is comfortable and has less folded bulk than a lawn chair. Exercise judgment shopping for camp furniture. Small-diameter tubing doesn't hold up well except for children. A chair that becomes rickety gets dangerous to sit in. Wooden-frame camp equipment seems to last better. It develops an "old" look after a bit of weather, but you can rejuvenate it by rubbing in linseed oil at the start of every season. You'll be surprised how many years the wood keeps its fresh appearance.

Take care of webbing and canvas on your camp furniture. Once a year, at the end of the season, scrub it down with very mild detergent or with baking-soda solution. Let the material dry thoroughly before storing. (Keep the tag that comes with your camp furniture. Some fabrics shouldn't be washed with detergent.)

Whatever you choose, allow room in your packing for furniture that lets you relax in comfort. Fatigue takes the fun out of camping.

No thoughtful camper travels without a flashlight. If you have extra money to spend, buy an electric lantern with sealed-beam or fluorescent lamp. Such lights are limited. For reading or that sort of after-dark relaxation, you have to carry extra batteries. Most campers therefore save their battery lantern for an emergency.

The gasoline lantern seems better suited for camp "rest and relaxation" lighting. Of course, you carry fuel for the lantern, but the same kind of fuel probably powers your camp stove. It's a white, completely unleaded gasoline distilled especially for lanterns and camp stoves. (The same fuel operates heaters for winter camping.)

The fuel for these lanterns is highly flammable. Observe these precautions. (1) Never haul an unsealed can of fuel. Leave the unfinished can with a neighbor when you break camp. (2) Never smoke while you're handling this fuel, either filling the lantern or lighting it. The same goes for operating a stove with this fuel. (3) You can't help spilling some fuel when you fill a lantern or stove tank. Carefully wipe it all off, preferably with a paper towel that can be thrown away. (Don't accumulate gas-soaked rags.)

(4) Don't store this fuel in your basement or garage. Buy enough for a trip just before the trip, and get rid of what's left when you return home. The stuff is explosive if it heats up in a corner somewhere. (5) When you do travel, transport the fuel in a trailer, at the rear. The further from the car, the better—in case someone bumps you.

Plan well and you'll incur little discomfort as you camp. You don't have to forego many of the comforts of home. No, you can't take a shower in your tent. Nor can you climb into the bathtub for a long soak. But you can bring along a washpan. Heat some water on the camp stove or over the campfire, and you can take a comfortable and refreshing sponge bath.

Or, find a campground with showers. Many state and national campgrounds include a shower house. Consider this when you line up where to spend your camping time. Some operators tack a slight extra charge onto the overnight fee if you use the shower house. If you enjoy freshness, it's worth it.

Whatever you do, don't give up your own concept of comfort and convenience just because you're camping. A little thought can make your camp life easier and like back home. Comfort, when you're out camping, is up to you.

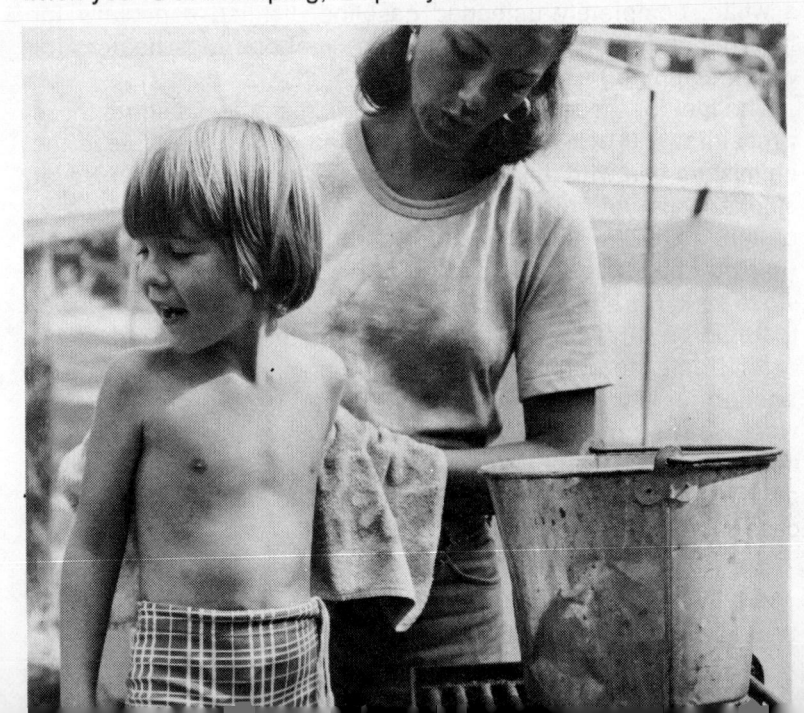

Chapter 4

Make Your Own Shelter

If you're willing to settle for minimal comfort, a shelter of sorts can be inexpensive. About all you really need to stay out of the rain is a generous-sized poncho. Learn to convert whatever you have at hand into a shelter that at least keeps the rain off. Whatever shelter you put together, though, should be tight enough to form a windbreak. Rain and wind together spell trouble for a camper.

In the pages that follow you'll see various kinds of shelters made from whatever is at hand. Pay as much attention to the principles involved as to the specific design. With this much help and a little ingenuity, you can improvise shelter from almost anything.

A 9×12-foot tarpaulin makes a handy staple if you might get caught in bad weather away from shelter. The exact size isn't important. It could be 10×10, or even 8×8 feet. The 9×12 is common and inexpensive.

To go with the tarpaulin, buy about 100 feet of good 3/8-inch rope. In nylon rope, settle for 1/4 inch. Why so many feet? With that much rope you can shape and hang your tarp shelter almost anywhere you can find a tree or two. One long rope lets you adapt to almost any shape the surroundings happen to be. If you can't manipulate one long rope, make sure all the pieces you have are at least 20 feet long. You need a minimum of five of them.

The tarp you buy should have eyelets sewn in solidly. The best material is duck canvas, water-repellant of course. Don't buy plastic ground cloth for this purpose. It can do the job in an emergency, but does not allow the comfort a canvas tarp can. For one thing you have that problem of perspiration. Plastic next to you or over you simply is not comfortable. The hotter the weather gets, and the more humid, the more discomfort you experience. You need a material that can breathe.

Also, plastic seems to tear much easier than canvas if it happens to snag. Once the plastic has ripped, a tear migrates rapidly. A tarp can grow tattered and worn through years of use. Yet, unless you apply an awful lot of pressure, a torn place won't go much further than where it starts.

You can make a tarp lean-to quickly and easily. The simplest version consists of about two-fifths of the tarp on the ground and the remaining three-fifths reaching diagonally up to and over the top pole. You will find more comfort where a bit of the tarp drapes over the top pole or rope. Let this front hood or valance stretch outward slightly beyond the floor's front edge by guying it with strips of rope.

A crackerbox shelter (photos) takes three crosspoles or crossropes. One goes on the ground and two at the top. The tarp forms a long, square hut shaped like a crackerbox with the front out. The front edge of the floor is staked, just like for a lean-to.

Set up the shelter with its back toward the most likely winds and rain, which come from the west in summer. Facing the east, the lean-to gets morning sun that helps dry out dampness. Be sure to include a ditch around the shelter for drainage.

47

You can fashion your own pup tent from a tarp. This pup tent even has a floor.

You start with a single rope stretched between two trees or between two guyed poles, about 2½ feet off the ground. Drape the tarp over that. Let the ridge rope rest at one-third, and a back-edge pole at another third (see photos). That leaves a third of the tarp for a floor.

Stake the two free edges to the ground, but not for their entire length. If you leave 2 or 3 feet on each end unstaked, you can fold closures. Stake down about 6 feet leaving 3 feet on each end of a 12-foot tarp. A tarp with several grommets along each edge stakes best.

Orient your shelter so one side is toward rain or wind. Hence, align the ridge rope or pole north and south. That puts one side toward the west. Dig a trench along each edge of the shelter.

The trenches carry water spilloff from the tent sides. Once you know how broad the tent bottom is you can dig the two trenches before you even stake the edges. Let the sides overlap into the trenches. That way water can't seep under the edges to wet the tent floor. This is doubly important when you're in snow.

Once you stake the tent, restretch the rope the shelter drapes over. Raise both ends if necessary. Make the sides as tight as you can.

Now about the end flaps. Pull both ends down and tuck them inside the shelter. Lay heavy stones on the parts that overlap inside. The tighter you can make these end flaps, the less wind or rain can get in. Leave one side of one end open as an entrance and exit. Once inside, you can close it against insects, animals, wind, and rain.

Trench across both ends. Connect the trenches on all four sides. At the lowest point, dig a drain sluice so water can leave the trenches. You want drainage, not a moat.

49

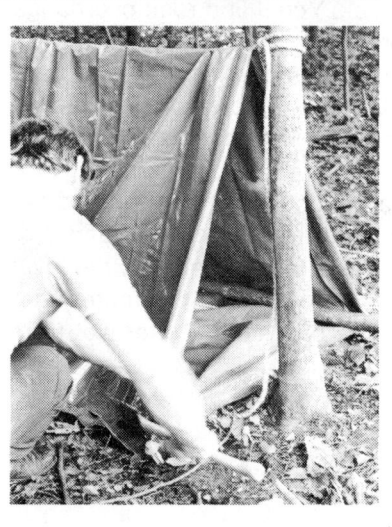

You'll find many natural shelters in the wilds if you look. However, stay away from trees. Sheltering in a hollow tree can be very dangerous; they attract lightning. You've probably known from childhood never to shelter under any tree standing alone in a field. Broad-leaved trees in the woods are some shelter from a quick rainstorm, but they drip a long time afterwards.

Try for a cave or overhanging rock. You'll find rock overhangs along streambeds, where erosion has undercut large rocks. Be careful, though. Look the whole situation over. Beware the danger of a mudslide bringing the hill above down on top of you. Thin-stratum shale can be particularly treacherous. Whack the overhang a few times with a stick before you crawl under.

One other caution about overhangs along a creekbed. In areas prone to flash floods, you could trap yourself. Watch rising water intently near where you have taken shelter. If the level begins rising more than an inch every 10 or 15 minutes, get out of there fast. Climb up above the overhang. Better wet from rain than drowned.

Tramping around, you'll find plenty of old barns and buildings you can use for shelter in an emergency. No farmer is likely to object to your stopping in an abandoned barn long enough to miss a thundershower. But think twice before you stay over. Once the immediate danger has passed, take a walk around. Look especially for No Trespassing or Posted signs. Both mean KEEP AWAY. Even without the signs, hunt up the owner and ask permission. That avoids the embarrassment and pique of being ejected later.

Observe caution around old buildings, too. Snakes shelter from the sun in them. You could break a leg falling through a rotten floor. Heavy wind might tumble a roof on top of you. Old houses usually are empty because they're not safe to live in. Treat them only as emergency shelter.

You can build a small and effective emergency lean-to from poles and tree branches. Two such lean-tos make a roomy pup-type shelter. The photos on the page opposite show how to proceed. You start with one eave pole between two trees. A forked pole propped from the ground supports the eave pole. Lean three shorter poles against the eave pole to establish pitch from eave pole to ground.

Then you need two or three stringer poles on the pitch poles, extending from one side to the other. These support the roof you will thatch from leaf-covered branches. The smaller the diameter of your pitch and stringer poles, the better. A 2-inch diameter is enough for the eave pole. A 1-inch diameter is better for stringers.

The stringer poles can be lashed to the pitch poles, or propped with equal-length forked sticks (photos). The lowest stringer can be staked.

Start thatching at one end, along the ground, and lay branches toward the center. The butt end of each branch goes upward, and the leaves downward. Let each generously leaved branch overlap the one preceding and let a portion of each branch overlap onto the ground. Before you quite reach the center of the first row along the bottom, start at the other end and lay another row along the bottom toward the center. At this point, dig the drainage for the rear of the shelter, and let the lower rows of leaves extend into the trench.

Lay branches to the center until finally one large leafy branch caps the row. If you study this arrangement, you can see that water would tend to flow toward the outside edges from the center branch.

Now start a second row of leafy branches a little bit higher on the stringer poles. Work toward the center from each end as before. Let this second row overlap the lower row sufficiently that rain landing on it drains on down to the ditching trench.

Next comes a third row and a fourth row. The tips for the top row stick out beyond the eave pole. If you can see daylight as you look at the finished lean-to from underneath, add another whole layer of thatching. Start at the bottom exactly as before, and put another layer of rows on top of the first one.

One warning. In many wilderness areas today, you're forbidden to cut underbrush. Save this shelter for an emergency. You might avoid trouble or even a fine.

53

If you've been able to drive to your camping destination, there's always this way to sack out for the night. In some vehicles, it's comfortable. In others, you'd probably rather sleep in a bag on the ground.

If the car seats are vinyl, or some other not-very-porous material, you'd do well to put towels or blankets under you. Otherwise, you'll have that same dampness problem detailed on pages 38 and 39.

Plan ahead for comfort and convenience and you probably won't end up having to do this.

Chapter 5

Keeping Dry

Dampness stands out as a serious enemy of comfort in camp. You've already seen some ways to protect yourself from wetness with tents and other shelters. You'll see more in this chapter.

Rainstorms are not the only source of dampness that can plague your camp. Moisture accumulates for any of several reasons. It really isn't much worse than it would be at home; but you notice it more because you're cramped into a smaller space and you're more dependent on what you have with you. If clothing or bedclothes get a little damp, no matter what the moisture source, you suffer noticeably.

Condensation is one major culprit. The coolness of woods at night, the same phenomenon that causes heavy dew, spirits moisture into your blankets with uncanny persistence. To stay comfortable, you must stay dry. You have to keep after every possible source of moisture and dampness constantly.

Rainstorms first. You cope best with them when you know they're coming. If you carry a radio, some local station usually has long-term weather reports—for example, what's expected tomorrow. But you need your own eye attuned to weather signs.

Easiest to recognize is the thundercloud with lightning in and under it. Such clouds generally move west to east. In some parts of the country the direction is from southwest toward northeast, and in others it's from northwest toward southeast. Heavy winds often precede storm centers like these. Once the wind starts, you can expect rain within the next 10 minutes. If you spot a cloud like this, tie things down.

You might experience extreme calm—an almost airless period—just before the storm breaks. In that case, you'll find thunder and lightning heavier than in a storm center accompanied by wind. A yellow-green appearance to clouds suggests you watch out for tornadoes. Hunt a ditch or hole to lie in if a twister does come through. *Don't run!*

A halo around the moon presages rain in a day or so. In colder weather, a large-diameter halo signals ice crystals in the air, and you can expect snow or colder weather within the next few days.

Some old weather "sayings" are surprisingly accurate. The one that goes "Rainbow at night, sailor's delight; rainbow at morning, sailor take warning" works rather literally. The reason: A rainbow is the prismatic reflection of sun on water droplets falling to earth. A morning rainbow naturally appears in the west because the sun is in the east. So, you can expect that rain in the west will move toward you.

Here's another clue. Rain that forms morning rainbows usually is a soft rain, not a storm. But it can last a long time and leave you plenty wet before it's through.

Another weather ditty goes "If the evening's red and the morning's gray, this is the day to make your hay." That's because a red sunset signifies dust in the air, and you probably won't see rain the next day. The second verse of the same ditty goes "If the evening's gray and the morning's red, the ewe and lamb will go wet to bed." This holds because morning sun seems red through a humid atmosphere. Clouds and fog form high in the air. Precipitation often follows in the next 6 to 12 hours.

These predictions in recent years have become subject now and then to peculiarities, especially around cities. Thermal pollution in the atmosphere creates some dire effects in our weather. Nevertheless, when you see these signs of rain, prepare. If it doesn't rain, you're still okay. If it does, you're ready.

Don't let a little rain spoil your outing. If your tent has a dining fly or awning, set up under that and continue with meal preparation or whatever. You can also buy an awning and erect it so it partly covers the tent and extends in front. It comes complete with five poles and the necessary guy ropes and stakes. It expands the space in which you can keep dry.

Digging a drainage trench should be part of setting up your tent. Ten minutes before a rain starts is a poor time to start ditching. The trench should be about 3 inches deep. If you set up on a hillside, you might want the trench deeper along the uphill edge of your tent—maybe 5 inches. Expand the trench to include your awning.

Dig a sluiceway at the lowest point. Arrange worktables, picnic tables, blanket line, etc., so your drain trench doesn't empty among them.

Never let anything inside your tent—table, lantern, person, or whatever—touch the material of your tent during a rain. That brings on "bleeding." Moisture on the outside gathers at any point of pressure on the material and seeps through there. This can happen even from someone touching a finger to the cloth while it's wet. The same thing occurs if a tree limb or bush outside contacts the tent. In close quarters, trim back brushy limbs.

Once a leak has started, water continues to seep in at that point. There's not much you can do to stop it. When the rain quits, shrinkage of the tent fibers reseals the spot. The tent will not leak there next time it rains—unless it's touched again.

To keep a bleed from dripping in the tent floor, take your finger and "lead" the water down to a drip pan near the floor seam. Just wipe your finger straight down the tent material. Stop before the bottom, or you'll guide the water too far down for a drip pan to catch it. Where your finger stops, the water stream will stop, form a bubble, and then start dripping there. That's where you set the drip pan.

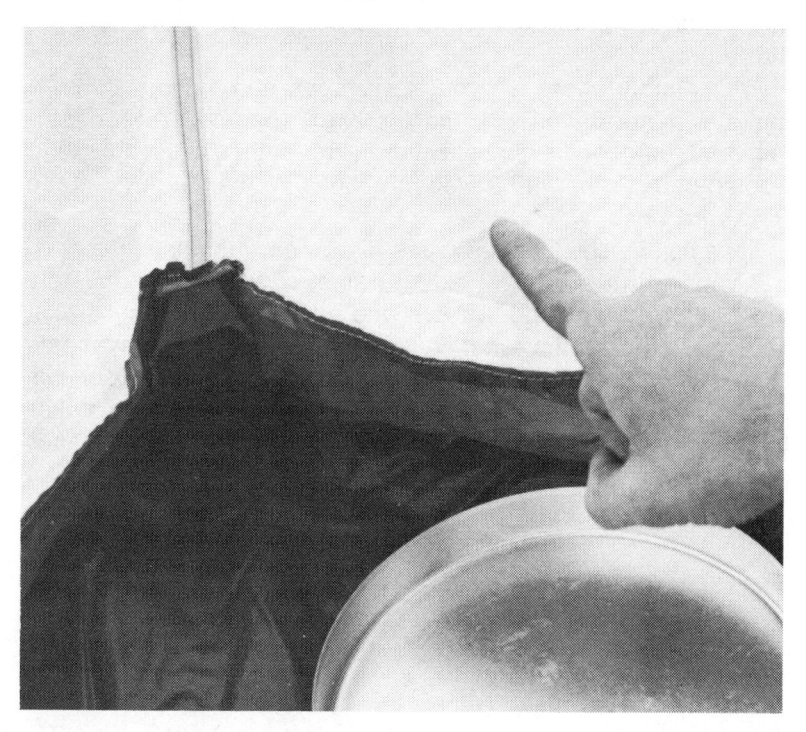

Heavy winds can be the most destructive force to affect your camp. But you can deal with damaging wind. Try to discern what direction a hard wind is coming from. Even when a weather front approaches from the west, you can't be sure its winds are going to obey the rule. During a thermal inversion, you're just as apt to experience wind from the northeast as from the southwest.

Immediately check all your tent ropes and stakes. Be sure tent stakes are driven at an inward angle (pages 24–25). Ascertain that guy ropes fasten securely to both stakes and tent. Don't battle storms with frayed guy ropes. Add extra guys on the windward side.

Take up any slack in guy ropes. That's easy if you use sliders.

If your tent has a freestanding frame, add a couple of safety guys before a big wind. Stretch one guy rope to the northwest and one to the southwest. If you have plenty of rope, play it safe and also put one northeast and another southeast. Four will hold your tent down in almost any wind. If you don't have stakes for these extra ropes, tie very low to nearby trees. That makes a solid guying arrangement.

Tie down your window flaps before a rainstorm. Inside the tent may get close, but better slightly stuffy than very wet. Zip or tie your tent door too. Mosquito netting will not keep out moisture, even in a soft downpour. In a blowing storm, it's a sieve.

Here's a special trick for high wind. Your 9 × 12 tarp makes a versatile windbreak. Once you're reasonably sure from which direction the wind is coming, quickly set up a V-shaped windbreak that streamlines the wind right past your tent. Three trees and four ropes do the job nicely. One tree forms the vertex of the V. Tie the four corners toward the other two trees.

You can do the same thing, although not as easily, with three poles from your dining fly, some guy ropes, and a few stakes. Set up the center pole and guy it in the direction you expect the wind from. Set the other two up with the tarp forming a V leading past your tent. Guy each pole with two ropes and two stakes.

You need a windbreak like this only in severe wind. It's trouble to set up; but it can help keep your tent in position if your forewarning of heavy wind leaves you time to set it up.

In the battle against moisture, two things most critical are clothing and bedding. Of the two, bedding probably is the more important. Daytime activity keeps you warm, even in damp clothes. At night you're quiet and body heat tends to drop anyway. That's the worst time to have dampness next to you. You'll end up chilling. Dampness can be very unhealthy.

Try not to let dampness accumulate. You already know to keep several layers of blankets between you and vinyl or rubber-treated materials. If moisture does get into your tent, wipe it up immediately with paper or cloth towels. Don't even let it evaporate inside the tent.

Every day that's possible, air the bedclothes outside. Try never to roll them up without airing. If you do break camp early and roll up your bed without airing it, open it up as soon as you make your next camp and hang out to air. On days that are rainy, spread the bedding inside your tent for at least an hour or two.

Best of all is to let bedclothes air in sunlight. The sun kills mildew and bacteria, and helps deodorize perspiration spots that could eventually smell soured.

Back home after a camping trip, put your sleeping gear through a large industrial-type washer. Use a deodorizing water softener in the final rinse. Or, wash twice and put the softener/deodorizer in the wash water the second time. Tumble it dry or almost dry, then spread it for a couple of days in the sun.

Keep wet clothes out of the tent. String up a rope or hang them on a limb. Leave clothes hanging in the sun until they're absolutely dry. Wring them out first and they'll dry quicker. Turn them a time or two during the day to make sure all sides get sunshine.

For transporting, put wet wear into plastic bags. Don't let their dampness reach blankets or other wearing apparel in the car. Save the plastic bags you buy ice in. They're waterproof and make excellent carriers for swimwear or clothing the rain has soaked. On the morning you break camp, put damp towels in plastic bags along with any other damp apparel.

These hints seem unnecessary and self-evident to anyone who has done much camping. But if you're new at the game, you'll be astonished at how insidious dampness can be. The best thing you can do is keep everything dry. Second best is to dry wet things as soon as possible. Third best is to store wet things in a way that they can't dampen anything else.

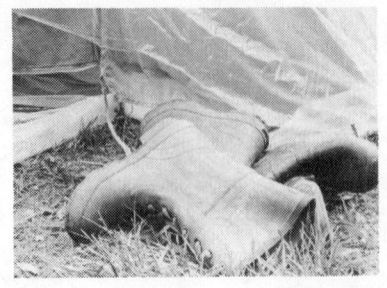

You or the kids track in a lot of moisture with bare feet after walking in dewy grass. Keep a towel outside the tent door for wiping feet. Impress on everyone the importance of not allowing dampness into the tent or bedclothes. If someone traipses to the restroom or bath house at night or during rain, they must dry off their feet or remove wet footwear *before* coming inside.

Don't run around with wet socks on. Treat your boots for wet-weather wear, or you'll ruin them sloshing around in wet grass and mud. Rub neatsfoot oil into the leather and the seams thoroughly. Don't soak the shoe in the oil, however. Saddle soap rubbed into the seams helps boots shed water. More important to the life of your boot, neatsfoot oil keeps leather conditioned and prevents drying and cracking.

Don't dry wet shoes or boots over the fire. Heat is detrimental to the leather. Admittedly, there will come an occasional time when you need to dry them in a hurry. If that's the case, go ahead and dry them near the fire; but don't place them so close they scorch. You only want to dry them out, not cook them. *Immediately* afterward, rub them thoroughly with neatsfoot oil. Otherwise they'll be permanently damaged and soon will need replacing.

Here's another good way to handle chores on rainy days. Cover up your wearing apparel with a rainsuit. It's inexpensive. You can buy a clear plastic rainsuit for under $10 at most sporting goods stores. Fancier ones cost upwards of $20.

If you take care of it, the low-cost kind does an excellent job. The point is, it keeps you dry and you don't have to wear wet clothes into the tent. In camping, there are times you simply cannot avoid being outdoors in the rain. You needn't be uncomfortable from it.

If you don't like the idea of the rainsuit, try a poncho (page 45) or a raincape and hood. Anything that keeps you dry helps you keep the rest of the camp dry too. You can't reiterate enough how important it is to keep all moisture outside your tent.

You must believe by now, if you want to stay healthy camping, one key criterion is that you stay dry. However unimportant you may think this admonition, a bit of experience will persuade you. Staying dry is prerequisite to staying comfortable. Becoming wet and chilled may not be the only path to discomfort, but you almost certainly cannot stay comfortable while wet or chilled.

The cooler the weather, the more serious this is. Even with temperature in the 70's and 80's, prolonged exposure to dampness brings on maladies you may be unaccustomed to.

Whatever else you do, stay dry. Keep your entire camp as dry as you possibly can manage.

Chapter 6

Staying C-o-o-o-l

You may think keeping cool is a problem when you don't have your air conditioner. Perhaps it is. But you can employ quite a few tricks to improve your comfort in hot weather. Nature provides many ways of her own to keep you cool. All you have to do is take advantage of them, and add a few special efforts of your own. This chapter may suggest a few ideas you hadn't thought of.

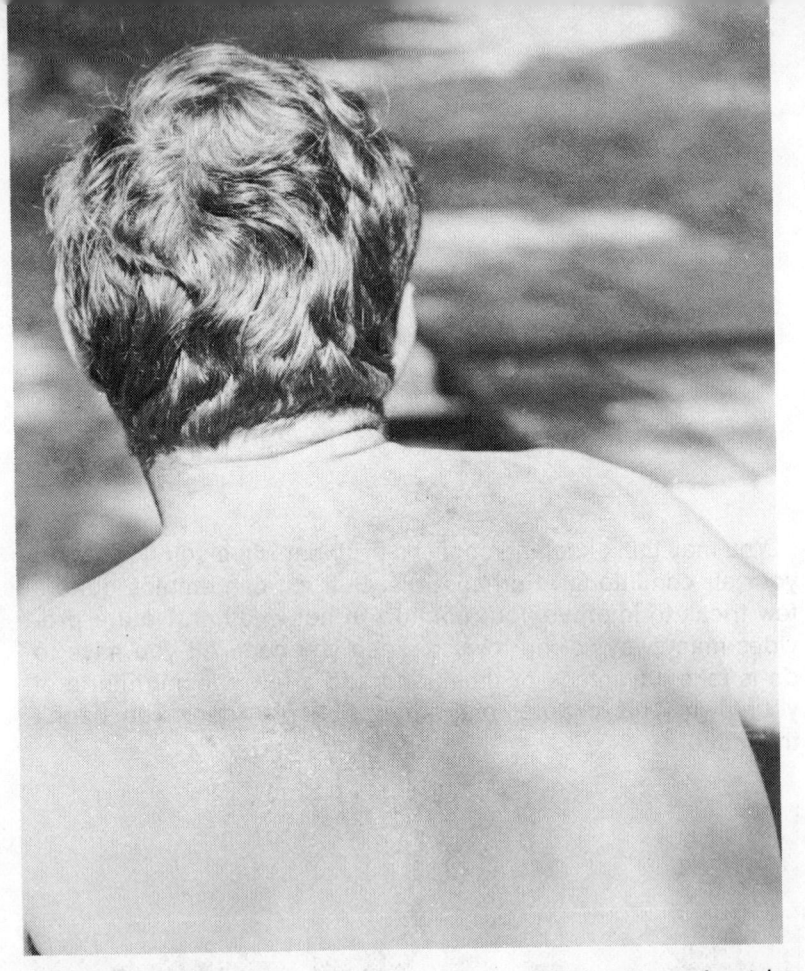

Nature's prime way of taking care of you in extreme heat is through your sweat glands. When you perspire, the moisture evaporates; and that evaporation cools your skin. If your skin can be kept cool, you stay cool.

Persons who perspire freely are seldom overcome by heat exhaustion, unless they dehydrate (run out of body water to perspire). Those who don't perspire well have a little more of an overheating problem. Never apply anything to your skin that prevents perspiring, because you should not inhibit your natural cooling.

The best advice on the matter is: do whatever you can to stimulate sweating on a very hot day. If humidity is high, evaporation won't be as rapid, and you won't cool as well. But you need all the body cooling you can get and perspiring is the handiest.

Proper cooling through perspiration and evaporation consumes water. Your body gives up a lot of moisture during hot weather if it's cooling you properly. In the process, your body also loses a lot of salt, which somehow has to be replaced. Lack of salt hastens the symptoms of heat prostration or heat exhaustion (page 77). When your body doesn't contain enough salt, it can't absorb water you drink the way it should. Your sweat glands can't produce enough perspiration to cool you.

Make sure you eat plenty of salty foods. Some people fail this, complaining it makes them thirsty. That's the very reason to take salty foods. Your body needs the extra water to cool you well on very hot and active days. Actually, unless some health problem limits your intake, you should add extra salt to your regular food—more than you use for seasoning. Additionally, you can take salt/dextrose tablets as a supplement to salt in your diet (the dextrose adds energy).

Finally, a special hint for hot days. Drink water, not soda pop. You can take in moisture either way, but your body absorbs plain water far better than it can the moisture in soda pop or beer. Where children are involved, you'd be wise to handle soda pop as an occasional treat rather than an all-the-time drink. Water does more good, and helps a lot to keep you and your family comfortably cool.

Nature's second best cooler is the breeze. Learn to take as much advantage of it as you can. For example, the higher you camp, the better the breeze. You naturally get more breeze in open spaces than if hemmed in by trees. Setting up camp for the night, consider prevailing breezes. Situate your camp so you're not cut off from breezes by proximity to trees or brush.

Some breeze stirs almost constantly. If you don't believe that, look at tree leaves. Something keeps them moving; it's the wind, however mild. You can decipher the direction of any breeze, however slight. Put your index finger in your mouth and wet it thoroughly. Don't merely wet it, but hold it there until it's warmed. Then hold it above your head. The side that first feels cool indicates the wind direction. The coolness occurs as the moving air evaporates the moisture.

If your tent has end vents, orient them so every little breeze blows through. Most tents have at least two windows. Align them so the breeze comes in one and out the other. These efforts to cool the inside of your tent surprisingly, even with minor breezes.

Most breezes are westerly. With side windows, face the tent south. With end vents or a window at the back, face the tent east. If the wind shifts, reorient the tent.

Take advantage of whatever natural shade you can. If you place your camp wisely you can have the ideal—morning sun and afternoon shade. That shade means a lot toward keeping your tent cool inside.

Even artificial shade can do a world of good. A popular accessory nowadays is the dining fly or awning. You can also set it up separate from your tent, where nothing interferes with the breeze from any direction. If it's feasible, put the awning a little farther away from woods or brush than your tent is. Or, find a position where the late afternoon sun throws shade onto and under it. A little extra thought given to shade accomplishes wonders.

Here's a little known technique you can use to cool the breeze through your tent awning or dining fly. Wet some towels and hang them at the breeze end. Some clip-type clothespins do the job if you have no other way.

The object is to hang the wet towels in a position that whatever breeze there is blows across them. This is a primitive form of air conditioning—a type once used in offices. Evaporation of moisture from the towels cools the air that blows across it. This technique doesn't do well on days when humidity is high, because evaporation is slow. But it helps on days that are simply hot without being overly humid.

The biggest aggravation is having to wet the towels every hour or so. But when you're hot and suffering, it could be worth the trouble.

Play it smart. Save your exercise and hardest work for the cooler times of day. The ritual of siesta during early afternoon in hot countries is not laziness, it's plain good sense. Locate the coolest spot in camp, and settle down for reading, napping, or just meditation. Two hours of inactivity can leave you feeling twice as chipper during the late afternoon and evening.

If perspiration on your skin doesn't cool you enough, soak a close-fitting T-shirt with water and the evaporation cools you. If you're a person who doesn't sweat much, this may be the only way evaporation cooling can help you.

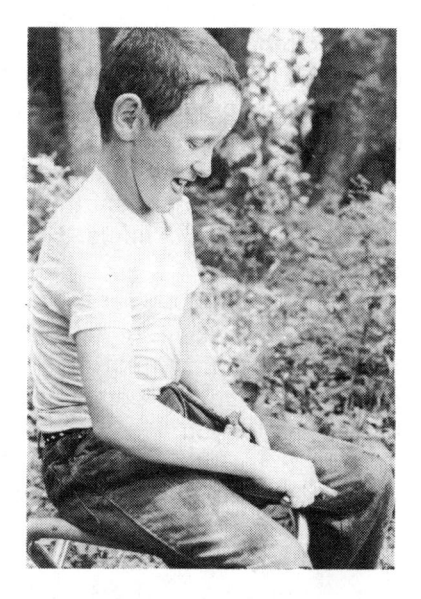

Don't use ice water on it. The shock harms the average body more than it helps. The water from a hydrant or faucet is okay. You can even use water that has been sitting and seems warmed up. It's not the temperature of the water that cools you; it's the evaporation from the close-fitting shirt. You could do the same thing with a wet towel.

The clothes you wear certainly affect your comfort in hot weather. Unless you keep a shirt wet and damp, as described on the page preceding, loose-fitting clothes cool better than those that fit tight. The reason is obvious: air is more free to circulate around your skin and provide that crucial evaporation. A loose-weave cotton shirt has more to recommend it in summer than synthetic fibers. However, some synthetic knits let the breeze in.

If you like shorts, wear them. They or a comfortable swimsuit can help make your hot days easier. But don't forget that shade aids evaporation. Direct rays of the sun heat your skin faster than evaporation of perspiration can cool it. A loose shirt or blouse shades you.

Keep these principles in mind. You'll be a little more comfortable in camp than you otherwise might.

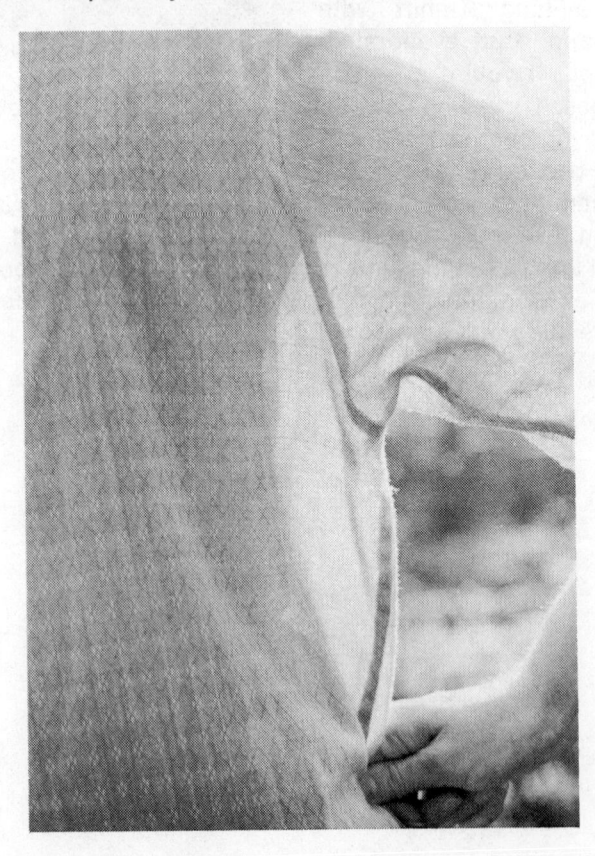

The sun can overheat your scalp very quickly, and do a lot of damage. Keep your head covered when you have to be out in the sun for any length of time. Your hair shades your scalp a bit, but not like a large, well ventilated hat can. You may chuckle at some hats you see, but they keep their wearers cool and safe. Don't laugh. And don't worry a bit if someone laughs at the hat you wear.

The larger the brim, the more the hat protects. But don't be talked into buying one of those crownless large-brim contraptions. They shade your eyes okay, and that's some help. And they keep the sun off your face and shoulders. But they don't keep the sun off your scalp and you need that protection in particular.

Panama straw hats are exceptionally cooling. And a hat of any light color does far better at cooling than a dark one. The light color reflects more, whereas darker colors tend to absorb heat and retransmit it to your cranium.

You'll encounter two real dangers outdoors in the sun. One is *sunstroke*. The other is *heat prostration* or *heat exhaustion*. Symptoms are not the same, and you must become familiar with both. Everyone in your camp should also know how to treat either one.

A sunstroke victim often complains of a headache first, and sometimes nausea. Then the face flushes very red. The victim may faint at this point. The skin grows very dry, because perspiration stops. Temperature goes high and the pulse pounds violently. The red face and heavily thumping pulse signify danger.

Sunstroke can be fatal, because of the extreme body temperature. Cool the victim down the fastest way you can. Hurry to the shade. Pour cold water over the whole body, even ice water if you have it. Soak wrists in ice. Put the victim in a creek, pond, or pool if one is handy.

A sunstroke victim needs a doctor's attention as soon as you can manage it. But first get that temperature down.

The symptoms of heat exhaustion manifest themselves early enough for prevention, if you only recognize them. The victim feels weak and nauseated. The face grows very pale, and pulse very weak and rapid.

In advanced stages, the victim may act chilled. Treatment is the same as for shock. Get out of the sun. Cool the wrists and forehead, unless the victim shows signs of chilling. Have the victim lie down with feet up; wrap him in a blanket if necessary.

Let a conscious victim take water slowly. When he can swallow, let him take salt/dextrose tablets. Don't force water or pills into the mouth of a semi-conscious victim; they could strangle a person. Recovery upon cooling and replacing body salt is almost miraculous. The victim begins feeling better within minutes.

The safest way to handle heat exhaustion is by avoidance. Be sure you and your camping group get enough salt, enough water, enough rest, and enough cooling. If anyone sweats a lot, be sure they take extra water and extra salt. They should rest a little more often—sit in the shade and cool down.

Here's another way to keep cool. Camp somewhere you can swim a lot. And then do it.

Be cautious of sunburn out in the water. Until you're used to it, swim for five or ten minutes and then lie in the shade for a half-hour and cool off. Then swim a little and cool off some more. A good swim following a siesta perks you up for the rest of the day.

Keeping cool is merely a matter of using natural cooling devices nature built into your body and into your surroundings. Supplement those with good judgment and a few tricks of your own, and you'll be one of those campers who seems cool and comfortable all the time. You'll be the envy of campers who swelter because they don't really know how to manage natural cooling.

Chapter 7

Ways to Stay Warm

Polar-bear camping can be a ball if you're up to it. Preparing entails more just than getting the equipment together. It takes conditioning to withstand the chill and cold you'll encounter. Proper clothing and camp gear have their place. But your own acclimatization has much to do with your ultimate comfort.

Winter is not the only time you could be cold. You run into chilly days and cool nights in summer camping. Campers in recent years have noted a growing proportion of unseasonably cool weather.

Staying warm bears similarities to staying cool—in the sense that nature provides certain mechanisms to help you keep warm. Some are built into your own body. Others you'll find in the wilderness if you know where to look and what to look for. Showing how to utilize these, along with the manmade warming devices you can take along with you, makes up the bulk of this chapter.

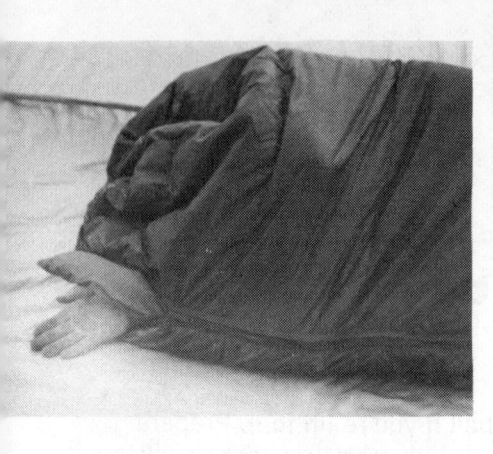

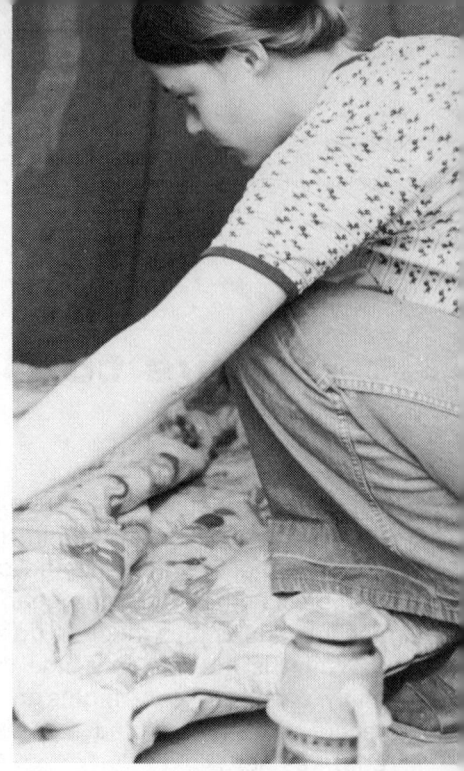

The two worst enemies of comfort when you're camping in cool or cold weather are *dampness* and *wind.* If you haven't read Chapter 5, do so before you read further in this chapter. Many of that chapter's suggestions apply here, because you can't stay warm in cold weather if you can't stay dry.

In particular, your bedding is more critical than in ordinary weather. Your body generates its own warmth, plenty for the most bitter weather, provided you supply some means of keeping the heat close around you. That's what your bedding does. Several layers of blankets or a down-filled sleeping bag holds this warmth in. What happens is, your body warms the air trapped between the bag or blankets and you. The layers hold the warm air, if the material on the outside doesn't let heat escape.

Hence, your sleeping bag should have a tightly woven outer covering that makes a good windbreak. The inner materials should be more loosely gathered so they trap a lot of air. Soft cotton flannel or a soft blanket next to you holds air your body has warmed. An outer layer of duck, drill, or nylon keeps the cold wind out and the warmth in.

The procedure pictured here is so important, it's repeated. You absolutely must air your bedding at least an hour every day. If you can't air it outside because of rain or inclement weather, do it inside the tent. With several sleeping bags or blankets, air them one at a time if that's all the room you have.

The point is to get them spread and aired, so perspiration moisture that has gathered (and you'd be surprised how much does, even in cold weather) dries out. Don't trust the feel. Moisture permeates the millions of little air traps in good bedding. You wind up chilled, even though neither you nor the bedclothes feel damp. Under no circumstances let your bedding go more than two days without airing of some sort.

If you're airing blankets rather than sleeping bags, spread them separately. Don't just drape the bunch over a line. All the little air sacs inside each blanket need a chance to purge of moisture. Hanging and airing is the only way that can happen. Air them individually even if you have to do it inside your tent.

Here's another idea to help you keep warm. Fluff your bedding vigorously before you climb into it at night. If your bedroll contains several blankets separate each and flutter it to let air in and around. With a sleeping bag, open it up and fluff fresh air into all its pockets and corners. This little bit of final aerating adds considerably to the coziness you feel through the night. (This works at home too. Try it.)

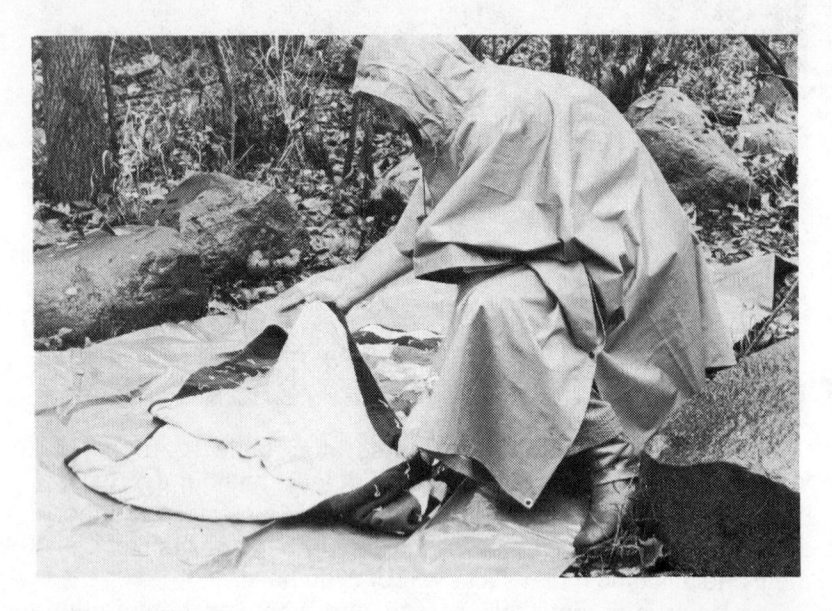

Sleeping on the ground during cool weather, you need plenty of insulation between it and you. First put down a ground cloth that's waterproof. This prevents dampness from migrating out of the ground into your bedclothes. Moisture has a way of doing that insidiously, as if drawn by a magnet.

The chill factor from the ground bothers sleep as much as the dampness factor. You'll need just as much or more cover under you as over you. So, on top of the waterproof ground cloth, add two or three layers of thick wool blankets or quilts. Wool has excellent ability to trap and hold air that has been warmed by your body. But don't sleep next to wool. Finish your underbedding with a folded layer of thick cotton blanket.

Smooth the ground beneath your ground cloth and underbedding. This helps keep wetness and moisture from creeping under your ground cloth. You won't get dampness through a waterproof ground cloth, but water under it definitely adds to the chill factor and your discomfort.

Better yet, put down a camp mattress. An air mattress will do; put blankets between you and it because of the perspiration problem (page 39). A mat with vinyl or leather on one side and cotton ticking on the other works best. The vinyl acts as a ground cloth, and the ticking lets your body heat warm the mattress stuffing.

This also keeps your body off the ground and absorbs some of the lumps underneath. Most important, though, is the insulating. You really must keep your body from getting chilled by the ground. A good mattress can mean the difference between sleeping comfortably all night and waking up chilled in the wee hours. You'd have to get up and build a fire or exercise vigorously for several minutes to get your body temperature back up to normal.

Foam rubber is not quite as effective as other stuffings for putting against the ground in bitter cold weather. Your body weight mashes out some of the air sacs that could otherwise hold warm air. However, foam is better than nothing. So take along a mat of some kind if you plan any cold-weather camping.

Plan clothing for cold-weather camping with some foreknowledge. A typical mistake is to wear too many clothes of the wrong kind. Wrapped too warm, your body sweats. When that dampness cools, your body becomes chilled. Even though you have on tremendous layers of clothing, you don't really stay warm.

Believe it or not, lighter-weight clothes are better for active winter wear. The secret lies in layered clothing. The layers act the same as blanket layers. The layers trap air, and your body heat warms it. An airtight outer layer prevents this warm air from escaping and keeps cold wind from infiltrating those air pockets. You stay warm.

You don't want too many layers. For sitting around idle, add a layer or two. When you're active, leave off the outside layer. This lets perspiration dissipate readily into the atmosphere. Your inner layers of clothing stay dry.

A pair of old-fashioned long underwear is good for much more than a few chuckles. Don't buy wool ones; they chafe. The most comfortable are made of cotton, with flannelette finish inside next to your skin. Don't buy them too small; let them fit snug but comfortable. This basic layer holds warm air next to your body. However, it also lets warmth through to subsequent layers. Don't wear nylon or Dacron next to you in cold weather.

Corduroy trousers make excellent winterwear. Their material traps and holds warm air, but fends off the wind that tries to chill you. Wear a soft cotton flannel shirt. In very cold weather, pick a wool shirt.

Over that, if you expect to sit around some, slip a wool knit sweater. While you're active, the sweater may be more than you need. But have it along to put on afterward so you don't cool down too quickly and catch cold. A cardigan type is handiest to get on and off, and you can open buttons near the top if you're too warm.

On the outside, you want a windbreaker. A heavy denim jacket does fair. Leather is far better, but more expensive. Vinyl jackets are exceptionally warm, but some can't take much wear. Consider a quilted nylon jacket.

A warning: Never use rainwear as your winter windbreaker. Moisture can't evaporate the way it should.

And a word of advice: Air your clothing just as you do your bedding. Particularly in cold weather, try not to wear the same clothing two days in a row.

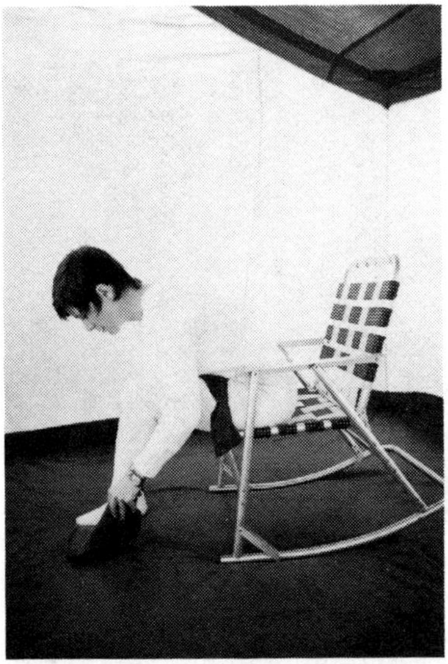

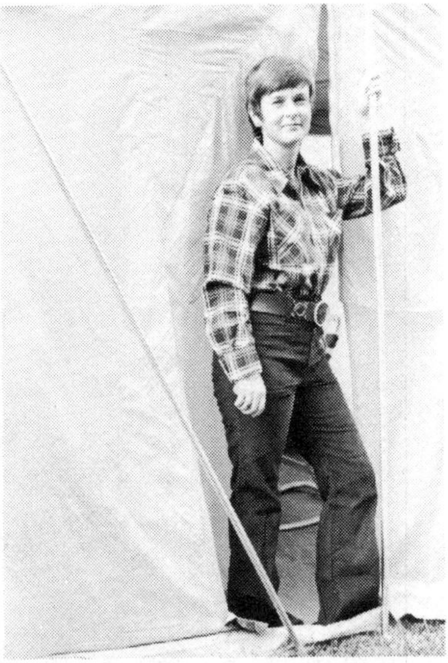

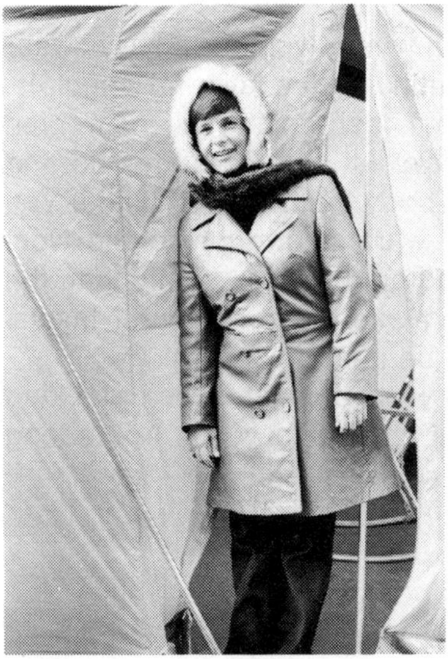

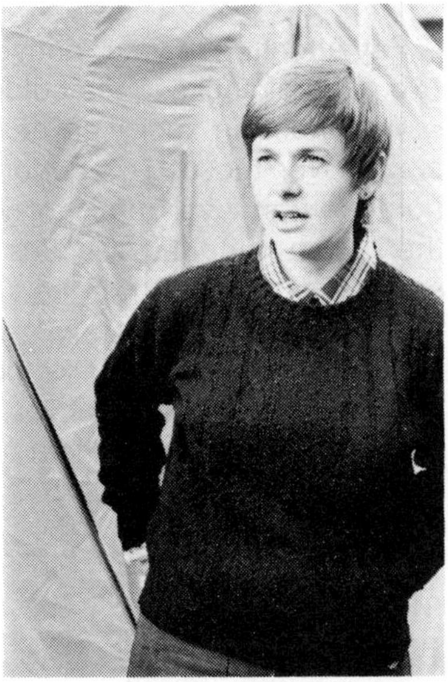

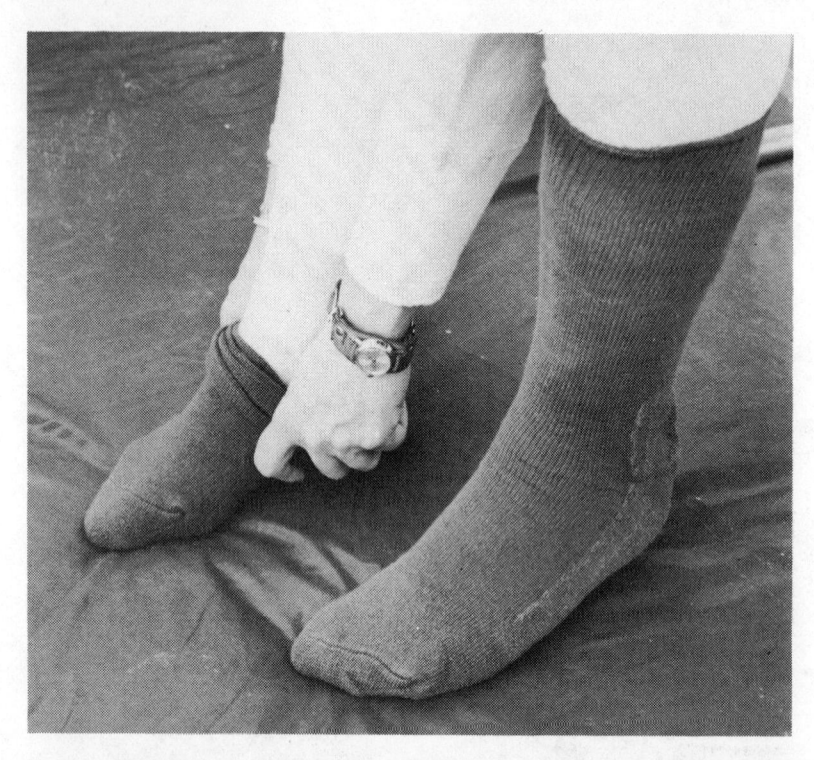

Pay attention to your footwear in winter weather. Always wear two pairs of socks in the cold, continuing the layering principle.

Warm cotton socks go next your feet, and a pair of woolen socks over those. The cotton socks let your feet breathe and hold the first layer of air for your body heat to keep warm. Yet, the cotton material also lets the warmth through to the wool socks. They in turn trap the air and hold it more tightly than the cotton socks do. That's why they make the better outer layers. Cotton socks over wool wouldn't be nearly as warm.

Absolutely avoid nylon or any kind of tight-woven stocking material. It makes your feet sweat and stay sweaty. In the long run, that leaves them cold.

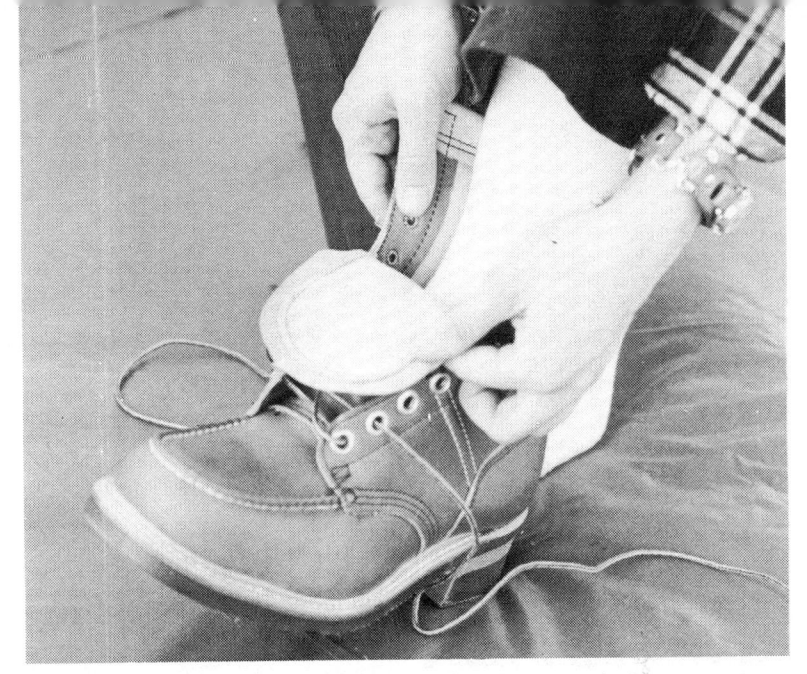

Buy your shoes for winter wear large enough to accommodate two layers of socks. A pair of good mountaineer boots combines comfort and warmth. The soles are thick, and usually the leather uppers are two-ply.

Pick a size that does not bind your socks tight. On the other hand, don't fit them too loose either. You don't want your socks to bunch up underfoot or around your toes.

Care of winter boots assumes more importance than of summer shoes and boots. Carry neatsfoot oil and saddle soap. Applied faithfully, these keep the leather pliable and waterproof. When you tramp through snow or wetness for a day or two, let the boots dry naturally and then rub in lots of neatsfoot oil. The best procedure is to let them dry overnight, and then rub in the neatsfoot oil next morning before you wear them. Don't dry your boots with heat. It's very bad for them.

Don't sleep with your boots on. They need the overnight chance to dry out inside. If you're sleeping out in the wilderness, keep them inside your sleeping bag, one in each bottom corner. They won't get so cold and they won't be exposed to moisture.

Wear fresh socks every day. If your feet perspire much, sprinkle a powder such as Zeasorb into the socks. Scatter some of the powder inside your boots at night. Next morning add some between your toes before you put your socks on. Dry feet are fairly easy to keep warm.

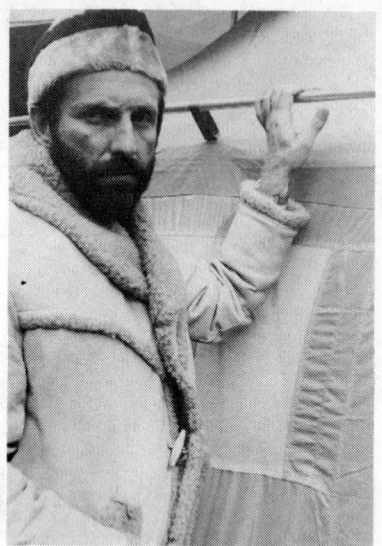

A lot of body heat gets away through the top of your head, believe it or not. A warm cap helps a lot to keep your body warm. Don't buy the kind of vinyl cap that makes your head sweat. You want something that keeps your head warm and yet allows perspiration that forms to escape naturally.

One secret to wintertime comfort and health in the outdoors: never become chilled. Once cold, you'll find it difficult to get warmed up without vigorous and extensive exercise. It doesn't take much experience outdoors in cold weather to reveal which extremities of your body get the coldest.

Wear whatever accessories you need to keep warm. Earmuffs may seem old fashioned; but if they keep your ears from frostbite, wear them.

You and your camping companions should learn to recognize the symptoms of frostbite. When an area of your body first gets cold, the skin begins turning red. That's because blood fills the capillaries right under the skin in an effort to warm the area. Frostbite begins one step beyond this. When an area becomes frostbitten, circulation in the capillaries ceases. The area turns white. When you see a splotch of white skin in an area of red, suspect frostbite.

Don't rub the frostbitten area. You could damage the skin and tissue. Instead, try to warm it naturally. Breathe on it, but wipe off any moisture that condenses. Cup a warm hand over a small frostbite area; that helps return it to normal body temperature.

If a hand or foot gets frostbitten, soak it in cool water. Never expose it to the fire. The warmth brings on considerable unnecessary pain and leaves tissue damaged.

Most important—as quickly as possible, get a doctor's attention.

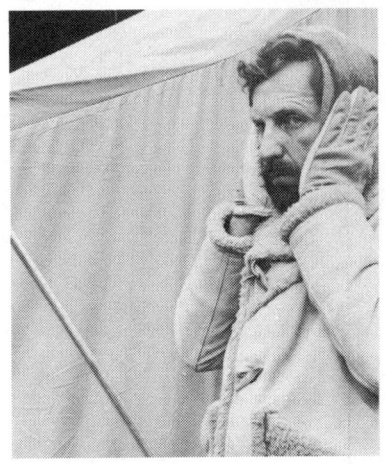

Hands may be difficult to keep warm. Of course, gloves are one answer, but not just any kind of gloves. The same principles involved in keeping the rest of your body warm apply to keeping hands warm. One layer of cloth holds air heated by your body. Top that with a tightly woven material to keep out wind. That's the formula for warm hands.

Leather gloves with the fur turned inside are among the warmest you can buy. The fur naturally gathers the warmth emanated even from cold hands. Some gloves have a lining like lamb's wool; that's excellent. The right combination is warm though lightweight.

Mittens are unusually warm, particularly leather ones, because they form a large pocket for warm air. When you're not doing work that requires your fingers, wear mittens, with thermal, wool, or fleece lining and leather outside, and with a snug elastic wrist cuff. Inside mittens, it's easy to keep your hands and fingers flexing and working. That's what keeps them warm the best, and mittens leave room for that. You can even make a fist inside to warm cold fingertips.

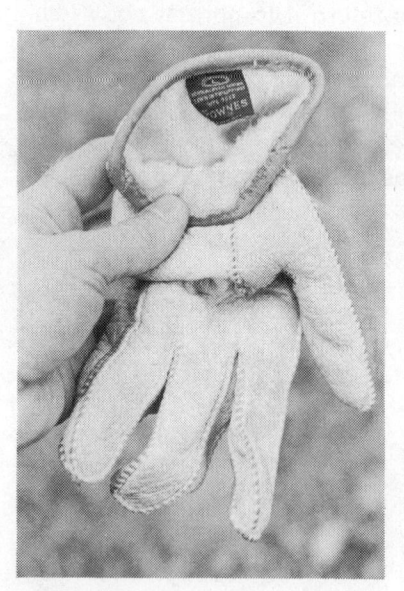

Something more popular now than formerly, yet still comparatively unknown, is the windbreaker cape. It wraps around your shoulders and fastens at the throat. Latchets further down let you wrap the material around you and fasten it. The cape fits over other warm clothes—the corduroy trousers, cotton flannel shirt, and wool sweater.

The best cape material is a close-woven—and perhaps waterproofed—fabric. Some capes are sewn from denim, but these usually allow too much wind through. Those made of plastic usually aggravate the perspiration and nonevaporation problem. Anything that lets you stay sweaty is not good for cold weather.

The poncho, you can see spread out on page 45. For windbreaker service, you put your head through the hole in the center and fasten the snaps on the sides. You can squat cross-legged on the ground with a poncho over you and stay surprisingly warm. Some ponchos have a parka hood that attaches for head protection. In a snowstorm, you'll really appreciate a poncho. It's waterproof *and* warm.

Exercise to keep warm. When camping outdoors in cold weather, plan some active chore every hour or two. If you have nothing else to do, get out and walk around—maybe hunting firewood. You can chop wood for the fire, jog, or get involved in sports. The exercise speeds up circulation. Exercise is the most practical and natural way to combat cold outdoor weather.

Be cautious of exactly how much you heat up. It's almost as harmful to overexert in wintertime as in summertime. If you work up a heavy sweat, you entertain a strong chance of chilling later. That lowers your resistance and brings on flu and colds. Don't exercise so strenuously that you pant heavily in cold air. You draw in too much cold air. When you're not used to it, that leads to bronchitis.

Even for exercise, dress warmly. Follow the principles already outlined. Layer your clothing, and adjust the number of layers to suit the vigor of your activities.

Don't forget nature's own heater. Sunshine can be mighty warm no matter how cold the day, if you block off the wind. Wear dark clothing, because it soaks up warmth from the sun's energy rather than reflecting it away from you as white clothes do. When you sit and rest, do it in the sunshine. Expose your feet and hands to the sun's heat, since they chill most easily. Let the sun warm your ears, or let it warm your hands and then cover your ears with them.

There's another natural way to warm yourself when you feel extremely chilled—a way few people know about or understand. This technique consists of deep breathing. When you begin to feel the kind of chilling inside that makes your teeth chatter and your body shake, start "forced breathing." Exhale as deeply as you can, pushing all the air possible out of your lungs. Then slowly inhale, and take in as much air as your lungs hold comfortably. Don't do this rapidly—just gently and slowly, in rhythm. If the air you're breathing is extremely cold, cup your hands and breathe from inside them.

Don't hold your breath. Breathe rhythmically in and out. What happens is this: extra oxygen—more than you're accustomed to breathing—enters your lungs and bloodstream. The oxygen warms your whole body from the inside. This is an exceptionally useful emergency measure when for some reason you can't move around to get exercise and build up body heat. You'll be astonished at how much this breathing exercise warms you.

Remember, only three elements cause you to chill: low temperature, wind, and dampness. You can't do much about the temperature. But you can ward off the other two.

In combating wind chill, don't overlook the natural windbreaks that surround you. For example, you can pitch camp near the base of a tall rock. That helps keep wind from you, unless you mistakenly pick a canyon with wind slicing through it.

Seek tall hills. Just as you pitch camp on top in summertime to take advantage of breezes, locate under the hill in wintertime to escape them.

Trees form a natural windbreak. In sparsely wooden country, set up camp on the lee (away from the wind) side of a small woodlot or even a bunch of heavy brush. Wind in the wintertime generally blows out of the north or northeast, at least the coldest winds do. You may be surprised how well a small clump of brush or trees breaks up wind currents that chill your bones.

Set up your own windbreak if you have to. A tarp spread into a V-shaped windbreak is highly effective in gale-force winds. Outback campers often carry two tarps. When the weather gets bad, they make one into a pup tent, like on pages 48–49, and the other into a V windbreak. The V streamlines the wind, shunting it around you. You feel very little of its chill effect.

You can build a "fort" with snow or brush. For the simplest brush windbreak, simply support a pole between two trees or bushes and prop lots of brushy limbs against it. If you have a good ground cloth or poncho and sleeping bag, roll up in the lee side of a windbreak like this. It can save you from freezing.

You can roll up comfortably behind a snow fort. Or, use the technique Eskimo dogs use. Just burrow into a snowbank and let the oncoming snowfall cover you over. The only danger is suffocation. Keep a stick with you, and poke a hole upward as often as necessary to keep an air shaft to the outside.

Take along an artificial heater if you have room in your gear. Propane heaters use lp gas bottles, which are efficient for camping. The bottles are small and contain a lot of heat energy. A camp stove warms several people gathered closely around it, in pretty bitter weather. The only drawback: be sure your tent is ventilated. Flames in a propane heater produce toxic gases that stay down along the floor of your tent.

Gasoline heaters are efficient. But consider the weight and quantity of fuel you have to carry along. Gasoline is more dangerous to transport than bottled lp gas. Gasoline cans are easily punctured. In an automobile accident, gasoline in the trunk of your car creates a deadly hazard.

Gasoline heaters operate like gasoline lanterns and cookstoves. You fill the tank with fuel and then pump it full of air. The pressure of gasoline flowing through a small nozzle vaporizes the fuel so it can ignite around the burner. You still have the ventilation problem inside your tent, because burning gasoline creates carbon monoxide. Very Important: When you turn off a gasoline stove or lantern for the night, set it outside. The afterflow of a gasoline burner produces carbon monoxide for quite a while. It could make you ill or even be fatal.

Catalytic heaters burn the same fuel as gasoline pressure heaters. The only difference is, a catalytic heater soaks the gasoline up into a catalyst which then is ignited. The catalyst glows very like charcoal briquets. You get a highly concentrated flameless heat.

The catalytic heater is probably safest of the three. There's no open flame, and no explosive pressure. You can't knock a catalytic heater over easily. Even if you do, fuel doesn't spill and ignite on your tent floor. But there are dangers. A paper or other flammable material dropped on the heater while it's glowing can ignite. You need ventilation the same as with any other gasoline heater, because of carbon monoxide. When you turn the heater off at night, set it outside awhile. Replace the steel plate over the catalyst when it's not burning. That keeps out foreign matter and rain.

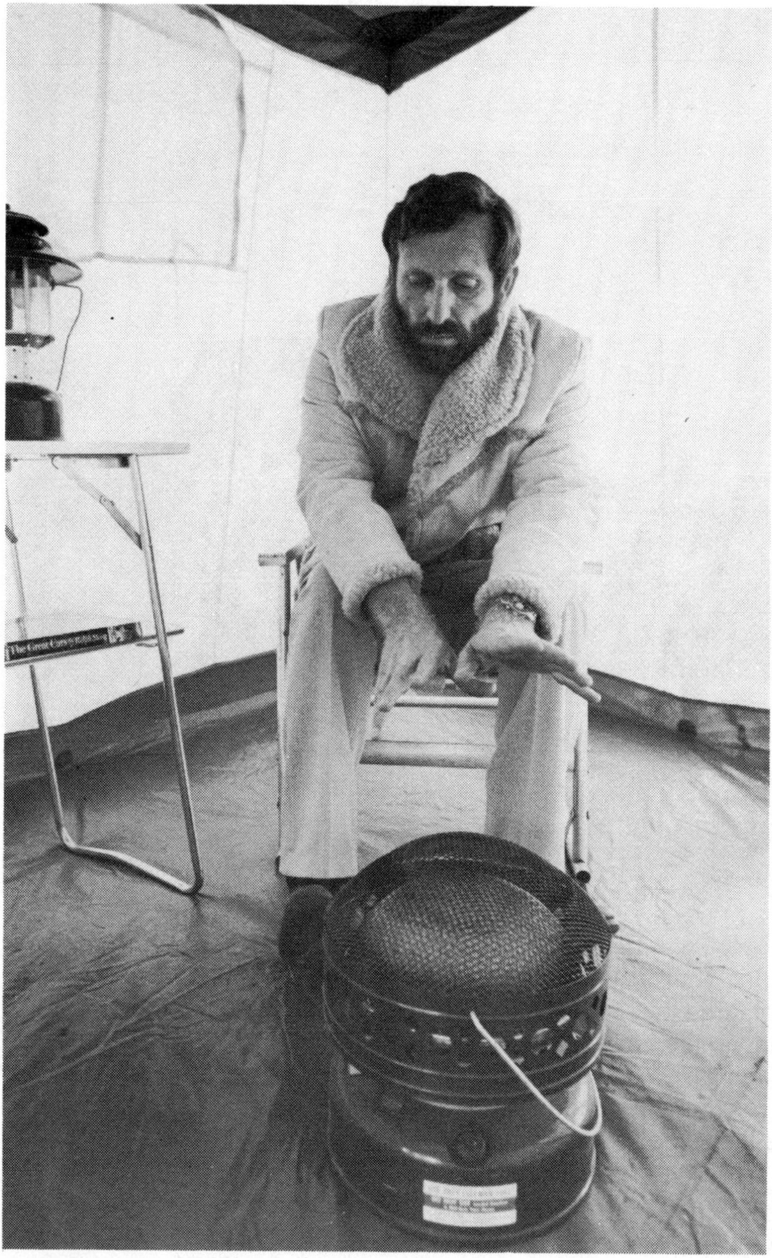

You can heat with natural materials too. Build a reflector behind your campfire to throw heat into your shelter. Put a couple of large logs or slabs behind your campfire even if you're camping in the open. The reflector increases the heating efficiency of your fire. You can have a smaller fire, burn less fuel, and enjoy greater warmth than if you keep building bonfires that consume all the wood within a half-mile.

The aim of this whole chapter is to show you how you can keep warm in cold weather away from home. Foremost, keep the wind out and keep dry. Then, get some exercise going. If you also need a fire, the next chapter shows that facet of camping comfort.

Chapter 8

Campfires: The Camp Workhorse

If there's one symbol of camping that's traditional, it's a campfire. Mention wilderness camping to many people, and that's the first thing that comes to mind. A campfire represents fellowship and romance. Oldtimers consider a campfire the key to contemplation and meditation.

But a campfire offers more than nostalgia and daydreams. A campfire has many practical uses. It can keep you warm, cook your meals, ward off insects, purify your water, help you fend off dampness, even scare away prowling animals.

One recommendation you should remember about a campfire, and this applies to all of them. KEEP IT SMALL. A bonfire has no practical use around camp. It too easily jumps out of control, and doesn't accomplish anything efficient. You'll see in the pages of this chapter how best and most safely to deal with campfires.

Gathering firewood makes a good cooperative exercise for the camping family. Do it when you first set up camp. Make sure everybody knows the kind of wood to gather. It has to be dry, and without loose bark on it.

Break the wood into lengths you'll use. Sort it according to diameter. You'll need kindling for tomorrow morning's fire, and plenty of larger wood for tonight's. Here are the five sizes: tiny twigs, smaller than a pencil; pencil-size twigs; finger-size kindling; half wrist-size; and arm size. For cookfire or reflector, a couple of logs 5 to 6 inches in diameter. Place the piles somewhere away from rain (under the car or table). It's important to keep your wood dry. Even the morning dew messes it up.

Rules in many forest preserves and national parks forbid picking up firewood. Dead wood that's part of the ground cover eventually decays and turns back to humus. Over the years this enriches the soil and nourishes growth. Besides obeying the rules, do your part to keep the wilderness lush and healthy. Don't pick up firewood in areas that have been marked with signs forbidding it. Haul your own in with you.

The danger of creating more fire than you want is high. A gruesome proportion of forest fires start when campers grow careless. The destruction is sickening. Every sensible camper must therefore know how to build, maintain, and quench a campfire safely.

The first step involves cleaning up the site on which you plan to build a fire. Loose leaves or brush within 4 or 5 feet of the fire can pick up sparks and ignite. Evergreen needles are exceptionally flammable. Clear a circle at least 10 feet in diameter right down to the bare dirt. When the woods are dry the fire itself dries out material within several feet. If you don't have a broom, use a stiff limb. Scrape ground cover away with your boots if necessary. Clear 10 feet in every direction (a diameter of 20 feet).

Never start a campfire without water at hand. If a quick wind picks up sparks or embers, the fire easily jumps even a 10-foot circle. Bring the bucket of water before you've started the fire. You need an immediate means of quenching satellite fires that spring up. In particularly dry weather, if the wind springs up suddenly, quench the main fire.

Now you can see even more reason to keep a fire small. You can't douse a large fire with one bucket of water. For even a small fire, you need two or three gallons. Keep the water nearby. If you use some of it for something else, like washing dishes, replenish the supply immediately. You just never know when a wind might come along and toss sparks.

If you don't have the knowledge, concern and good sense to handle campfires safely, you have no business in the woods. Our forests don't need heedless or thoughtless campers.

Camping in public places, you'll see many kinds of campfires. Few will offer much efficiency. The reason: few campers today know how to build and utilize a campfire properly. For example, on a chilly evening, someone builds a big campfire and then sits upwind of it. Why upwind? To keep the smoke out of their eyes. That's wrong and wasteful.

You can wring twice the heat from a fire one-third the size, thus burning less wood. Here's how. To alleviate smoke, select dry wood. That permits you then to sit downwind of the fire; heat wafts toward you instead of away.

Obtain even more benefit from your small fire by placing a large log opposite you. The log reflects the fire's warmth toward you. A fairly green log lasts longer than a dry one, but may induce smoke. However, if you stoke the fire with very dry wood, its efficient heat lifts minor smoke over your head.

One word of caution. Don't build your fire against a large fallen tree. That might smolder for days or weeks, eventually bursting into flame and starting a forest fire. Use only a short log—one that the fire can consume—as the backlog for your fire.

Lacking a large log, or the means to cut one, build a reflector from wood the size you burn. It's every bit as effective as a backlog, and offers other advantages. For one, it dries out wood that you can burn later in the fire. Then you replace the reflector logs with fresh ones.

You might be surprised how much warmth you can derive from a campfire built in the lee of a reflector like this. Keep the fire small and the wood dry, and the minimal smoke rises above your head. If you do have a problem of smoke in your eyes, try sitting lower, perhaps on a ground cloth.

Your campfire for cooking can be even smaller than for warmth. The object is to keep the heat concentrated in a small space right under the cooking pots. A spread-out fire loses heat into the air around the pot, contributing nothing to heating the food. That wastes fuel. Firewood is precious if you're buying every stick or carrying it a considerable distance.

To keep your cooking pots from blackening and to extract the most from your fuel, avoid flaming cookfires. Cook over hot coals burned down from very dry, hard wood. A thick bed of coals from a solid wood like oak or hickory can last 30 minutes or so. That's enough time for most cooking. If you find you'll need more time, feed in fresh wood at the outer edge of the coals, where the flames that stir up don't lap around your cookpots. Then, as the new wood forms coals of its own, rake those coals under the pots. You'll have plenty of heat under your pans continuously.

An exceptionally efficient cookfire for two or three cookpots can be laid between two medium-size logs. You keep the fire low and concentrated in coals. While you prepare the food for cooking, lay plenty of hard, dry wood between the two logs and let it burn down. Arrange the logs so the prevailing breeze goes right up the fire trench. The draft burns the wood efficiently and fans the coals hot during cooking.

Keep the bottoms of the pans within an inch or two of the hot coals. The closer they are without touching, the more efficient use they make of the heat energy developed by the coals. The sooner your food cooks.

You'll see campers all around you misusing their cookfires. They build a big fire and hang cookpots 6 to 8 inches above. The pots blacken, and dinner takes an hour or more to cook. The wise and experienced camper builds a small, sturdy fire and lets it reduce to a concentrated bed of hot coals. Cookpots are seldom black, and dinner is ready in one-third to one-half the time.

Feed your trench fire by putting new dry wood at the downwind end of the coals. As it catches, the flames lean away from the cookpots and avoid blackening. As the new wood forms coals, push them under the cookpots.

The logs support your cookpots, too. Keep the log diameters small. Remember, you want the cookpots within an inch or so of the coals. If you have pots of various sizes, separate the logs far enough that the pots fit down between. Then construct stick cradles to hold the pots above the hot coals.

Firemaking can be an art. When you understand the principles you can build a roaring fire in minutes. With poor technique, you waste a lot of time and wood. Follow these steps to build a trench cookfire between two logs, quickly.

For tinder, start with dry paper or very dry, decayed leaves. Slightly damp material won't ignite your first twigs. Wad this tinder together, but not tightly. It needs plenty of air to support combustion. Dried grasses from a nearby field ignite easily.

Next gather a large bundle of tiny twigs. They should be smaller than a pencil and very dry. Dead wood is not always dry. If a twig breaks with a sharp snap, it's dry. If it bends or splinters, it's no good to start a fire with.

Inexperienced campers try to build fires with twigs that are too large. Lay a lot of tiny twigs over your tinder. Pencil-size twigs go on top of them. They too must be very dry.

You're ready to apply the match. If there's much wind, use two matches together. Some campers carry a cigarette lighter for igniting campfires. Apply the flame to the upwind side of the tinder. If you don't know which side is upwind, because the breeze is so slight, use the finger-wetting method explained on page 70. The wind carries the flame across and through the loosely interlaced twigs and pencil-size kindling.

Once you have vigorous flame in the kindling, quickly add finger-size dry limbs, stacked in loose fashion. Don't use long pieces of wood for this step. The pencil-size twigs should now be burning vigorously, and should kindle the finger-size pieces. If you've been slow, blow on the coals. That usually stirs up enough heat to ignite the larger wood.

The next level of wood is about half the size of your wrist. Lay these larger sticks fairly close together right in the flames, yet leave room for air to circulate.

Once the half-wrist-size wood has caught well, pile on as much larger wood as you feel will give you a good bed of coals for cooking. If at any point combustion is slow, blowing or fanning can help. But don't expect green or damp wood to burn with any vigor.

Once the coals have burned down, keep the fire going by adding more dry wood regularly. Don't add it on top; feed from the ends. Notice the word *dry*. That's the only kind of wood that gives you the hot coals and smokeless burning that serve you best.

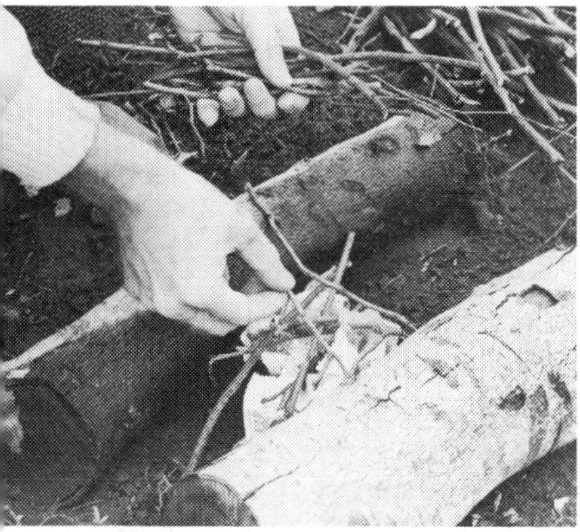

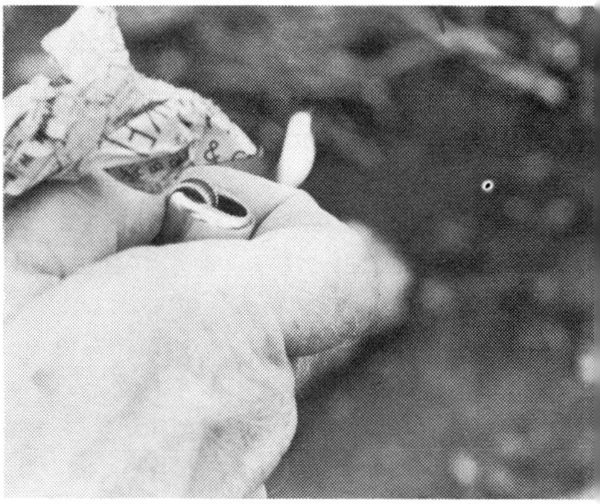

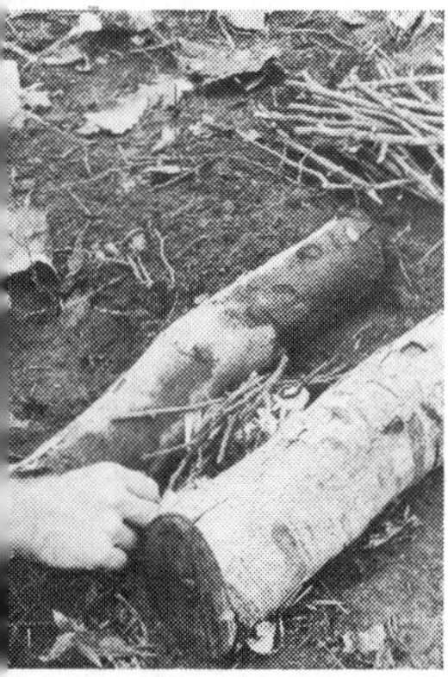

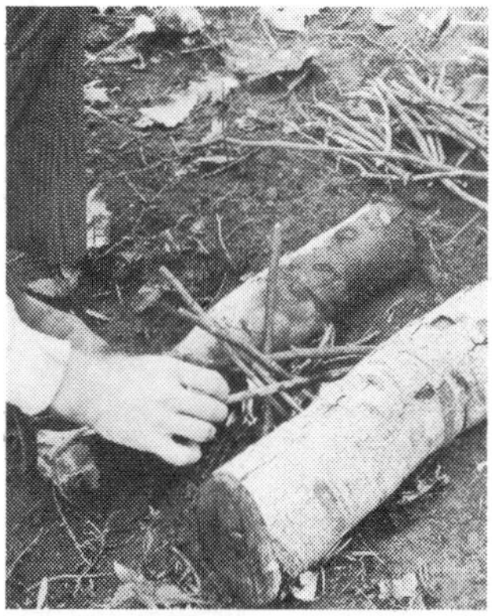

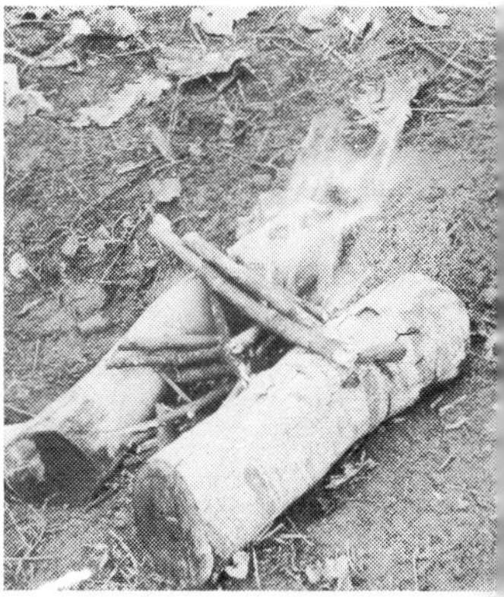

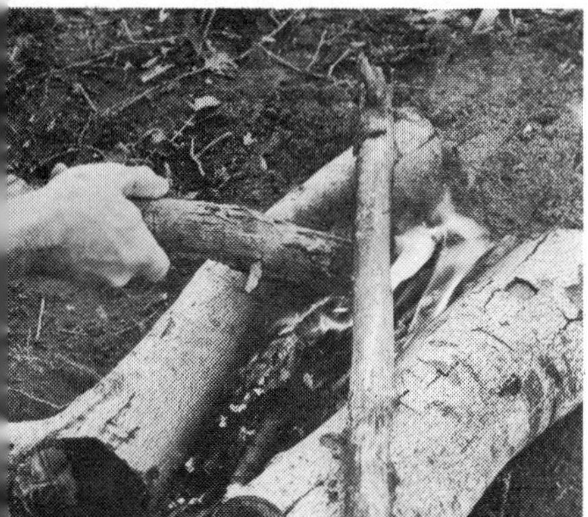

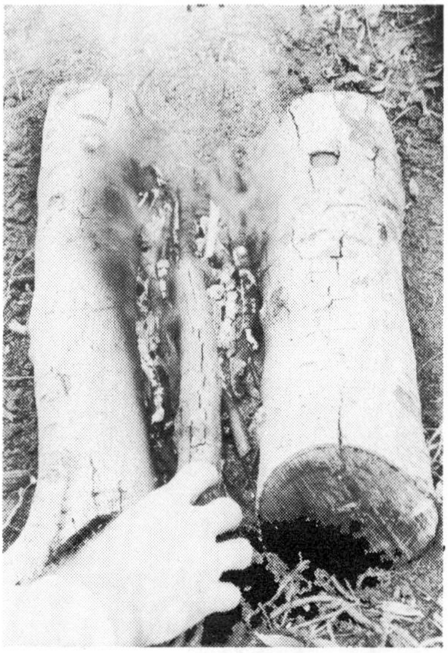

The grandaddy of outdoor fires is the *star* campfire. It takes this name from its shape. The flame sits in a small center, with wood fed in from five or six directions.

One factor is important. The wood must be very dry, so it burns easily. You can feed in sticks of wood like this the whole evening. You get total consumption of the fuel. The proper star fire generates no smoke, and heat from the coals in the center stays intense. Those coals make for excellent one-pot cooking. In front of a reflector, the star fire delivers effective two-person heating.

The steps to building a star fire are similar to those for building the trench cookfire. You start with a small piece of tinder and a bunch of very tiny twigs. The only difference is that you lay them in sunburst fashion, centered on the tinder. Pencil-size twigs come next. Break them a little longer than the tiny twigs, because they should overlap in the center. Again, lay these in sunburst or teepee fashion.

109

So far you've read a lot about keeping a fire smokeless by using dry wood. There are occasions you might want smoke. Usually that's when you're about to be eaten alive by mosquitos and don't have any insect repellant.

Green or damp wood produces smoke, but the wood may not keep burning either. A more dependable way is to strip handfuls of green leaves from the ends of twigs and pile them on the fire periodically. This produces more smoke than you and the mosquitos will want around.

Give some thought to which way the wind is blowing before you build a smudge fire. The rather acrid smoke may engulf your neighbors' campsites too. If the smoke is thick and the breeze brisk, your neighbors may not truly appreciate that you're keeping mosquitos out of their camp. Of course, you can always stop a smudge fire by adding very dry wood and no more leaves.

You can substitute moist leaves from underneath the top layer of ground cover. If worse comes to worst, and you can't find any moist or green leaves, you can soak dry leaves or even newspapers with water and apply them to create the smoke you want.

Just remember that smoke can be as unpleasant for you as for the mosquitos. But it does help thin them out.

You are not, in some parks, confined to campfires or your camp stove. Campgrounds often include grills in which you can burn wood or charcoal. Some have fireplaces suitable only for wood. These grills are for cooking. You can warm yourself by them, but that's not the most efficient use of your fuel. They concentrate heat upward, not outward.

The principles of laying and maintaining a fire in a grill or outdoor fireplace are the same as for a campfire. You may find fires a bit easier to start because of better ventilation. But it nevertheless takes tinder and small kindling. Use dry wood. Try to find hardwood logs, because you need hot coals just as with any other fire.

Charcoal works well in these grills. It burns clean and doesn't blacken the bottoms of your cookpots. Always cook over coals or embers, rather than over flames. Your camp cookware will take a lot less scrubbing. Soot on the bottom of cookpans seems to migrate to hands, faces, clothes, and just about everything in camp.

For cooking, there's no argument that a camp stove is cleaner and more convenient than a wood campfire. But there are dangers involved with these as well as well as with open campfires. You can circumvent many accidents if you just take the trouble to read and heed the instruction manual that comes with your camp cooking equipment. It explains how to refuel and lists all the precautions. When something goes wrong, the manual is even more important. That's when a gasoline or propane stove becomes dangerous.

With cans of gasoline, you have puncture-and-spill danger that requires much care and caution. Arrange blankets around gasoline containers if you can, so nothing in the trunk of your car or trailer can slip and puncture the can. Never transport an opened gasoline can. That's a sure invitation to soaking something in fuel and then igniting it accidentally with a match or cigarette. If you have a little bit of fuel left over in a can when you're through in camp, give it to a neighbor who's staying. Besides making a friend, you'll avoid later dangers.

Before you ever strike a match near a gasoline stove, look it over closely for any dampness. Wetness indicates new gasoline, maybe from a leak. If there is any, wipe it off carefully and thoroughly with a dry cloth or paper towel. One thing you absolutely do not want is a free flame fluttering around on your gasoline stove. This leads to an overheated tank and consequent explosion. Find how the gasoline got on the outside. It may have been when you filled the tank, or there actually may be a leak.

Pressurize the fuel tank with the little manual pump before you attempt to light the stove. Yet, be careful not to overpressurize, either. Some users always relieve the tank pressure completely when they first set the stove up. That way you start from zero pumping up the pressure. After the proper number of strokes, then go through the lighting procedure detailed in your instruction manual. You can safely add pressure to the tank later if it seems to be dwindling.

Most propane for camp stoves comes in 2-lb bottles. They're safe to handle, and easy to transport. Larger propane tanks are not unsafe, but some people don't know the simple rules of handling them.

For example, you never open the hand valve without the tank connected to a gas system. Make the coupling connections first. Purge the system by opening the stove burner furthest from the tank. You'll smell the distinctive garlic odor of propane when there's no more air in the gas lines.

Close the jet. Now check at all joints for leakage, BUT NOT with a match. That would be very dangerous. Instead, *feel* around the joints. Propane gas, upon contact with the atmosphere, gives up so much thermal energy that any metal it touches goes almost immediately to 40° below zero. You'll feel the coldness with even a very slight leak. If there's much of a leak, frost forms at the leaky joint. Wear gloves when you tighten a connection like this. The chill is so intense, it can severely frostbite your fingers.

Compared to wood, charcoal burns so clean that many campers prefer using it. You don't really need any kind of fancy grill, although one with ventilation operates more efficiently and burns cleaner than when you pile the charcoal in a pit on the ground.

You'll need charcoal starter fluid, a petroleum distillate somewhat similar to gasoline. It's not as dangerous as gasoline to use, but treat it respectfully. For example, if you try to light the charcoal and it fails to catch, pouring additional charcoal lighter on the smoking embers can be very dangerous. The mild "poof" explosion very likely will singe your eyebrows and might even be strong enough to burn you seriously. If you have that situation, light a piece of newspaper and toss the flame in before you add more fuel.

Best of all, put sufficient fuel on the charcoal before you attempt to light it the first time. Most people squirt on barely enough to cover the outer surface of the charcoal. Since charcoal is porous, it quickly soaks up the fluid so much that combustion is only superficial. Soak the charcoal thoroughly with the lighter fluid. Then, for good measure, soak it again. The fuel won't stay "wet" long on the outside of the charcoal; but it soaks in far enough to do a good job of lighting the briquets.

Never cook over charcoal while there's still a flame. The flames that flare up while the lighter fuel is heating up the charcoal to burning temperature only blacken your pots and pans. Wait until the charcoal has formed embers. In bright daylight, the charcoal briquets assume a gray ash appearance along the edges. At night, you can see the glow of the burning charcoal.

Once the charcoal has settled down to glowing, get your cooking utensils down as near to them as is practical—within an inch or so. Of course, if you're grilling steaks or other meat, 3 or 4 inches is more appropriate. The heat from charcoal is very intense. It's an efficient fuel for camp cooking, but it has considerable bulk and weight if you have to transport it very far.

Take the same precautions using charcoal that you do with any other campfire. Don't ever go away and leave it untended. Leave plenty of bare ground around it in case something spills and causes sparks, or a wind springs up and blows sparks out of the ember pile.

Keep a bucket of water handy, to pour over the embers when you finish. NEVER go away and leave the coals to die out on their own. Douse them, and then feel them. They should be cold and not warm when you leave them. There should be absolutely no smoke, because that means something is still burning.

Which leads to that one all-important rule of fires anywhere outdoors. NEVER FAIL TO QUENCH YOUR FIRE, and the entire area surrounding it, with water. Absolutely drown every last spark or ember in the ashes. Many damaging outdoor fires start after the camper has left the area. Fire can smolder in wood not just for hours but for days.

Pour water into the ashes until they're thoroughly saturated. Stir them like you were mixing concrete. Mix it up like a mortar, so you know every single bit of ash has been saturated with the water. Dig down, too. Fire can follow roots and buried limbs.

This all takes time, and an unbelievable number of shiftless campers are simply too lazy to do it. Don't be one of those. A change in the wind or some other unexpected occurrence could roll a hot ember into dry tinder. From there it doesn't take much to fan it into a king-size conflagration.

DROWN YOUR FIRE.

Chapter 9

Safe, Tasty Eating and Drinking

A gigantic picnic feast in camp marks the uninitiated. Or it characterizes the family group that shows limited concern for the comfort, convenience, and pleasure of whoever prepares the meals. Appetites are large outdoors. But meals should be simple and nutritious, with no fancy frills. That's not to say you shouldn't eat well and plenty. Just don't go the old "country dinner" route in which there's a staggering variety to choose from at every meal.

Plan meals before you even start the trip. Then you can lay in the exact groceries you need, in quantities you'll use. A majority of campers, even experienced ones, carry about twice as much food as they need. That's wasteful. Look through the pages that follow; they show the best kinds of food to take along for camping.

Meats are important protein sources for active campers. Fresh meats spoil quickly without refrigeration. So the next best thing for camping is to buy meats that don't need refrigeration.

Into that category fall canned meat products. They make good sandwiches with cheese or chopped up and made into "meat salad" sandwiches. Once they're open, you have to use them or in some way refrigerate them. Never take a chance on meats that have been out of the can more than an hour or so, particularly on hot days.

Frying adds a margin of safety against contamination, and a different taste. Many things you can do with other meats, including skewering for shish-kabob, you can do with canned meats. Cook them over the fire, broil them, fry them, or prepare them just about any other way you can think of.

Vienna sausages make a quick lunch if you like them. You can also buy deviled ham and canned meat-salad preparations. Again, don't trust these products more than an hour or so outside the can. Eat them or get rid of them. Even refrigeration doesn't suffice for salads that use mayonnaise, which spoils quickly.

Canned goods are a bit heavy to transport, and you wouldn't use them backpacking. You'd go for dried meats of the jerky type. Nor, if space and weight are considerations, are you likely to use products like canned hams. Yet, if you're planning meals for a large family, you can justify larger meat purchases. You can bake a canned ham and it'll keep longer. Nevertheless, for the sake of safety from food poisoning, even with refrigeration, use meat leftovers the very same day. After 12 hours or so, even in the cooler, you just can't be sure there's no contamination.

A smoked "country" ham, being cured, doesn't spoil easily. You can carry it for weeks. Keep it in a plastic bag after you've cut it, to keep flies away. Let it "air" for an hour now and then so it doesn't get damp inside the plastic. A whole ham feeds a lot of people, and you may not want ham for every meal. Pick the size rather carefully. On an extended camping journey, a smoked ham could be a good investment.

You can buy fish that have been smoked and won't spoil quickly. With it too, once having started cutting on it, keep it wrapped. Refrigeration isn't necessary. The curing extends all the way through properly cured meat.

Avoid certain meats for camping trips. Except on the first day out, wieners and bologna contaminate quickly. Their nature makes them highly susceptible to spoilage. They should be well packed in ice even that one day. Any that are uneaten the second day, even with refrigeration, should be pitched to the birds or otherwise disposed of. Never eat day-old hotdogs.

Steaks are out, too, except on that first evening. Unless, of course, you have a camp refrigerator. You can keep them under refrigeration a few days, but not in an ice chest or icebox. You can manage two or three days with dry ice. But that requires careful wrapping and storage—the dry ice can't be handled, and it evaporates soon.

Root-type vegetables suit camp cooking. Large round potatoes are a staple. They won't spoil for some weeks if you keep them cool and dry. The same is true of turnips, radishes, cucumbers, cauliflower, and vegetables like that. Anytime you cut into one and break its skin, keep it in a plastic bag and refrigerated. Carrots fall into the root category, although many people slice them up and treat them more like a green leafy vegetable (page 123).

Cooking root-type vegetables offers several choices. You can boil them, fry them, bake them, or roast them in ashes. Some people like turnips, potatoes, and carrots raw. Radishes, you always eat raw or put them in salads.

Clean all these foods thoroughly at home so you won't have that chore in camp. This also conserves water, in case it's scarce on the trip.

Clean these vegetables with the skin intact. That retards spoilage. If you have to cut out flaws, put those on top so you use them first.

If you have doubts how to prepare foods in camp, some camping cookbooks offer a lot of ideas. Copy down some of the best-sounding suggestions on 3×5 cards and take them with you.

Take vegetables in cans. The cans are extra weight and they're bulky. Yet, they may not take as much space per serving as some raw vegetables. Consider this tradeoff as you plan your camp menus.

Another problem is disposing of empty cans. Part of the mess that ruins camping areas are cans that unsavory people toss aside without regard for who's coming later. If you're not where cans go in trash barrels for park sanitation people to haul away, the least you can do is flatten the cans and bury them. That's still not the best answer but it's better than leaving them lie around to rust on the ground.

Cut the lids out of both ends. Put the can on the ground and partially flatten it. Slide the lids inside and flatten it tight enough to hold the lids. When you have a stack of these, bury them at least a foot deep, some place away from the campsite. It's the smallest courtesy you can show yourself and those who follow you.

Fresh green and leafy vegetables can be fixed up before you leave on your camping jaunt. Wash them thoroughly. Slice them into sizes convenient for individual eating. Pack them in an airtight container such as Tupperware.

Be sure the container fits into your cooler or your camp refrigerator. The colder you keep these, the longer they stay fresh and crisp. After washing them, shake them dry. A little bit of moisture keeps them from drying out in the box, but too much causes deterioration and spoilage.

Many campers prepare green peppers, celery, and carrots. Lettuce is best kept in its head and wrapped in a piece of plastic. The colder you can keep it, short of freezing, the better.

Backpackers go for freeze-dried foods (page 136). They are lightweight, and don't spoil easily. They're for sale in camping stores.

Right at the supermarket, however, you can buy less costly foods that do about as well. Examples: dehydrated soups in boxes or small packets. Dried and evaporated fruits are exceptionally nutritious and full of energy, and without the water and calories of their fresh equivalents.

Such dried foods are light to carry, take up little space, and have a slow spoilage rate. Even after the cellophane packages are open, spoilage retardants keep the fruits safe to eat for many days. They're tasty. They satisfy a sweet tooth without tooth-decay and calorie problems. Kids will usually settle for dried fruit after meals instead of candy.

If you shop around you can find a considerable variety of dried foods nowadays, from freeze-dried to sun-dried (like raisins). Investigate all of them. Try some at home. They're healthful, handy, and not expensive.

Pastry and bread mixes are lightweight and inexpensive, take up little space, and are great labor-savers for the camp cook. You can bake pies in camp, even without an oven. Put a piecrust mix in its pan, lean the pan against a fire reflector, and turn the pan three or four times. The pieshell bakes almost as smoothly as if it were in an oven. Pour in the filling. Plan pies that have some sort of topping—like meringue, which you can brown at a good campfire. You can cook up a delicious pie filling from dried fruits, and the pie doesn't even need strips of crust over the top.

Pancakes make excellent breakfast, or you can cook biscuits from a mix. The mix is a lot handier than messing with baking powder, flour, etc.

The same holds for cornbread, a perennial favorite in the wilds. Cornbread is a tasty part of a real woodsman's evening meal. Some people like cornbread with sweeteners, others prefer mixes without. If you shop around a little, you can buy either kind.

Puddings and gelatin deserts fall into the category of boxed mixes that offer tasty treats. You can carry fresh milk for puddings the first day or so in an ice cooler, or longer if you have refrigeration. Powdered milk won't spoil, and neither will condensed milk in cans. You can use puddings to fill pieshells you make from piecrust mix.

Saunter through the boxed mixes department in your grocery store. Project a little imagination. You'll find you can serve just about any kind of dessert in the woods that you can serve at home.

To go on those biscuits you make in camp, carry along jars of jelly, jam, preserves, peanut butter, etc. These are great for snacks. Peanut butter is virtually a staple, particularly with kids along. It packs tremendous quick energy, and it's a good source of protein. You can have peanut butter and lettuce sandwiches, peanut butter and jelly for the kids, peanut butter and crackers.
   Breakfast desserts of biscuit and jam tempt all but the most finicky appetites. Use jellies and jams as topping on pancakes. Mix them with pudding, for an unusual taste treat. You're limited only by your imagination.
   You can carry syrup to put on pancakes, but you might want to try honey instead. It makes a terrific sweetener, taking the place of sugar. It doesn't cause tooth decay the way sugar does. But its sweetness satisfies a sweet tooth and its dextrose is an excellent energy source. You can use it for making up jams and jellies on the spot with dried fruit you bring along.

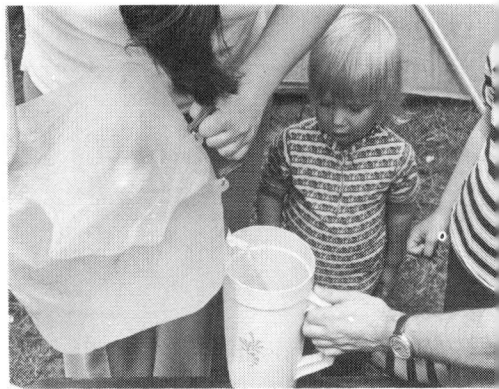

Beverages often become a problem on camping trips. Fresh milk sours without refrigeration. Most people won't settle for drinking water, even though it's truly the most thirst-quenching drink you can imbibe.

So, take along some freeze-dried coffee, tea in bags or loose, Kool-Aid, and Tang. All you have to do is add hot or cold water and you have a refreshing beverage.

Tea in the box beats tea in the bag. Not everyone can brew loose tea successfully. The secret lies in bringing the water in its kettle to a brisk, bubbly boil. Simmering won't do. Drop a half-teaspoon of dry tea leaves into a cup. Pour the superhot water over it. Don't stir; just let it steep. The tea leaves settle to the bottom. Stir in a little honey and—mmmmm.

Powdered or evaporated (condensed) milk answers the need for milk in camp. With powdered milk, experience has shown you'll get a better-tasting product if you mix two or three times as much powder per measure of water than the instructions call for. It works better for cooking too. If you like cream in your coffee, buy a jar of coffee "lightener." Mix up a combination of powdered milk and instant chocolate powder such as Quik. Add water and you have chocolate milk. Heat it and it's hot chocolate.

Shop for lightweight, compact powdered beverages. You can put together tasty drinks by mixing different kinds. Try Tang and strawberry Kool-Aid—unusually good. Ice from the cooler makes it tasty and refreshing.

Carbonated soft drinks are not a good camp beverage. They don't quench thirst nearly as well as water. They're impractical, besides. For the amount of moisture and dextrose energy they give you, they take up a lot of space and weight. If you're in the wilderness, disposing of cans or bottles creates a problem (page 122).

Carbonated soft drinks aren't good unless they're cold. If you have camp refrigeration, you're okay. But they occupy a lot of space in a cooler that could be used to far greater advantage for other foods.

If you can't do without soft drinks, buy them at a store near where you're camping. Some parks have machines near shower houses or the camp office. Let soft drinks be a once-or-twice-a-week treat for the kids, rather than an everyday thing. Direct them to healthier beverages—particularly water.

An ice chest is one common means of keeping camp foods from spoilage as long as possible. If you're camping in parks, you'll usually find plenty of ice available from machines. As you're traveling, there's ice at service stations. When you depart into the real backwoods, a good cooler keeps your ice for perhaps two days.

When you start your trip, you can help make the ice you buy last a little longer by putting in one or two slabs of dry ice. Don't put the dry ice next to food, as it freezes food solid. Keep the dry ice wrapped in paper, so you don't touch it. (Ever had an ice burn?) Special gel briquets that you freeze at home help for the first two or three days. Your ice lasts a bit longer.

One other caution about ice chests. Animals such as raccoons and bears break into them. Even the type with catches have been opened by smart animals (raccoons) intent upon plundering your food stores. Put your cooler inside the car or trailer for the night. Or, rig a sling and swing the chest from a tree limb out of reach (page 132).

Small portable propane or electric camp refrigerators keep milk, meat, eggs, even ice cream. You can have steaks in the freezer compartment. Freeze your own ice if you need to. It's still good, however, to have a cooler and ice with you. You never know when the refrigerator might quit on you or you might run out of fuel for it. You might end up some place with no electric hookup. If that happens, eat the ice cream quickly and rush the milk, meat, and eggs into the ice chest.

Safe and tasty water can become a serious problem in the wilderness. Carry as much fresh water with you as you can. Serious campers have a large water cask and keep it filled, even between camps. You never know where you might run out.

Boiling constitutes the surest way of killing contamination in water you find in the wilderness. Suspect water you procure from any strange spring or stream. You can usually find sources of water in the wilderness, if you know where to look and how to use them once you find them. You can melt snow into water to drink. But be sure you boil it. Snow simply melted has impurities collected from the atmosphere. It can upset your stomach and digestive tract.

Boil water at least 20 minutes at full boil. Let it set until the sediments settle to the bottom and form a scum on top. Scoop off the scum. Then pour off the water into another container, leaving the bottom sediment.

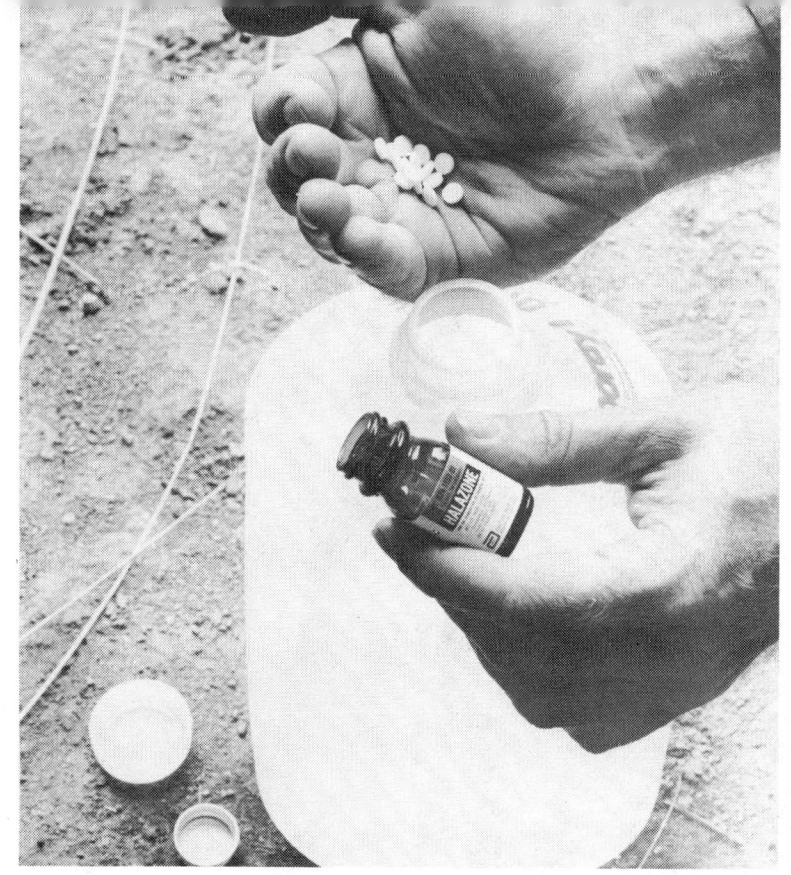

Even that isn't always 100% sure. For final assurance, always carry water purification tablets. You can buy a large size that purifies a gallon of water with only a few tablets. Or, there are "cup-size" tablets you buy in a drugstore. It takes quite a few of these to decontaminate a gallon of water, but don't hesitate to use that many. Better safe than sick.

You can also purify water with household bleach. Just be certain you follow directions. Chlorine bleach is harmful itself if you use too much. Here is the procedure:

Treat a gallon at a time. If you have a chance to boil the water, do so. At least filter it through a cloth to get the big sediments out. Then mix only THREE DROPS of chlorine bleach in the gallon of water. Shake it up, and let it stand for 30 minutes. Taste it. If you cannot taste the chlorine yet, put in six more drops of the bleach. After another 30 minutes, sample it again. Repeat this until the water finally tastes slightly of chlorine. Then it's safe to drink.

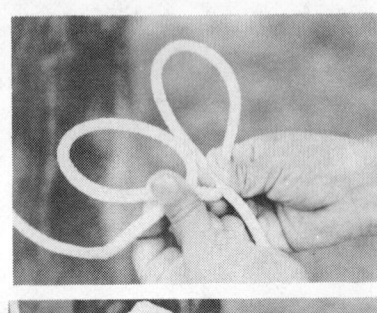

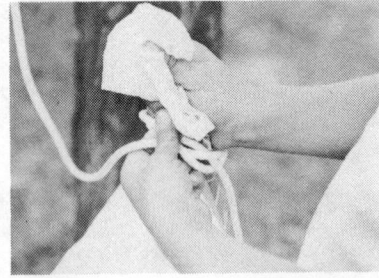

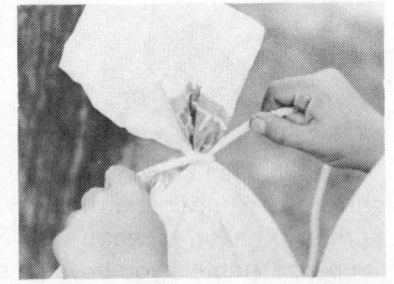

Keeping animals away from your food can become a major concern, whether you're in a national or state park or far out in the wilderness. This includes everything from ants to bears. A simple and practical way is to put foods in a bag and hoist the bag up under a tree limb. Don't pull it all the way up to the limb, or climbing animals like raccoons or possums will be drawn to it and might chew the rope through. Support it higher than a tall bear could reach.

You can use the bag you carry your sleeping roll or tent in. Toss your rope over a tree limb. Flip a clove hitch near the end. Slip the bag through the hitch and pull the knot tight. Hoist the bag and tie the end of the rope to a tree.

You can deter ants by spraying table legs with repellant for crawling insects. Or, set each leg in a can of water.

Chapter 10

Backpack Hiking In Comfort

Reaching camp, for most campers, involves driving down a few back roads. However, one type of individualist makes his way to where even four-wheel-drive outfits can't reach. That's the backpacker. You have to be a hiker. Your food and shelter go with you on your back. You learn early the meaning of weight and size. Every ounce rests on your shoulders. Every inch of unnecessary bulk cuts down what you can squeeze into your pack.

Yet, as a backpack camper, you needn't be uncomfortable. Modern packs and frames allow you to carry all you need. That doesn't mean just anything you might want, but enough to make your life comfortable in the wilderness.

If you haven't backpacked before, you need a guide as to what you should take along. This list comprises an individual minimum. Take things like camera and film only if they are significant to your trip. Add whatever items you know you need. Limit your pack ot 30–40 lb unless you're an old hand.

Foods	Hand axe
Halazone tablets	Whetstone
Salt/dextrose tablets	Waterproof matches
Cooking mess kit	Watch
Canteen, filled	Insect repellant
Folding plastic bucket	Calamine lotion
Knife, fork, spoon	First aid kit
Tiny radio	Nylon twine
Tent	Nylon rope
Sleeping bag	Soap
Ground cloth	Comb, brush
Poncho	Towel (2)
Clothing	Tissues
Compass	Toothpaste, brush
Pocketknife	Sewing kit
Sheath knife	

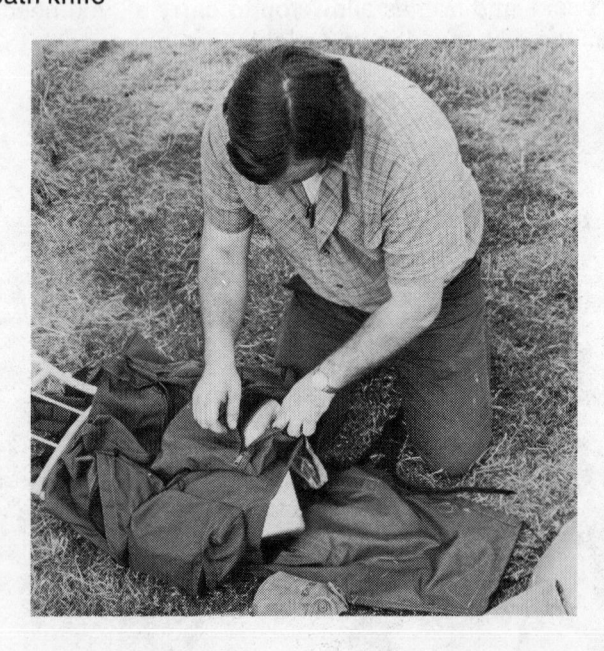

There are two alternate ways to arrange inside the pack. One way groups similar things together, such as food, clothing, etc., so you can find them easily.

The other way is to pack by the day. That is, you put one day's food and clothing in one layer. The next day's food and clothing make another layer. And so on. The final day's supplies go on the bottom. Items you need every day go on top or in outside pockets.

Outside the pack, on the frame, tent and ground cloth go on top. (When you stop for the day, you pitch ground cloth and tent first.) Sleeping bag and bedroll go on the bottom, just over your hips. This can help cushion the small of your back and alleviate some pack pressure.

Comfort and convenience are part of the game. You'll be lugging that pack some pretty tiring distances. Pack it however makes good sense to you, and memorize the order. You can then fit things back into the pack, even in the dark, without having to figure out the arrangement.

Undoubtedly the most popular development in backpacking provisions is freeze-drying. With moisture removed, ordinarily perishable food won't spoil. They're in a category with dried and evaporated fruits (page 124). Properly packaged, they last for a year or more. Even with the vacuum-sealed package open, spoilage is greatly curtailed. It's wise to keep dried foods in the package, though, to avoid contamination by insects.

Many backpackers make up their own special rations. Some have developed recipes for extremely nourishing "gorp." Here's a tasty recipe one experienced backpacker published in a recent issue of *Backpacker* magazine:

- 2   12-oz semisweet chocolate bits
- 2   8-oz butterscotch chips
- 1/2 cup honey
- 1/2 cup chopped dates
- 1/2 cup yellow raisins
- 1/2 cup Fini (Bircher Muesli)
- 1/2 cup chopped dried apricots
- 1/2 cup shredded coconut
- 1/2 cup cashews
- 1/2 cup walnuts
- 1/2 cup wheat germ
- 1/2 cup uncooked oatmeal

Melt chips in double boiler. Add honey. Pour over other ingredients in large bowl and mix well. Pour into greased pans to cool. Cut into hand-size chunks. Wrap in Saran.

Whether you backpack or camp from your automobile, you should carry two things: extra water and emergency rations. You can buy readymade kits of emergency provisions and survival tools. They fit in your car, pack, boat, plane, or however you might suddenly be caught away from home. A good emergency ration kit is usuable up to two years.

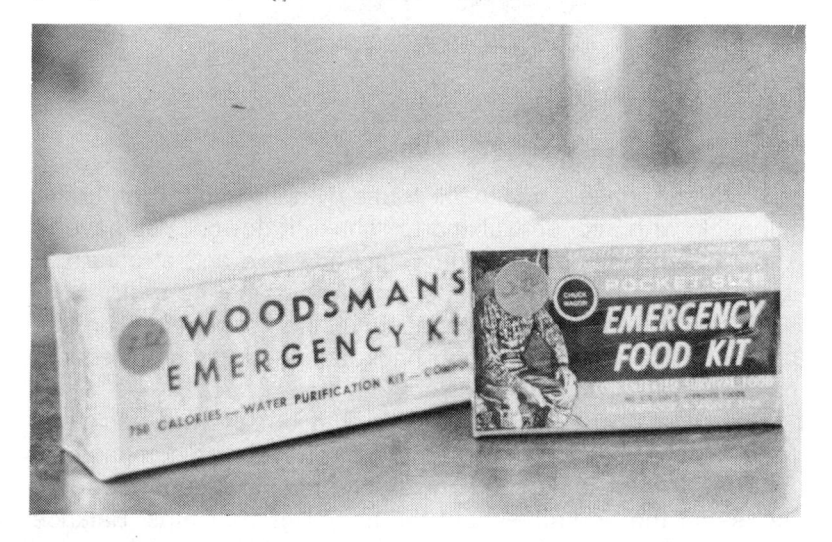

Also carry a small emergency first-aid kit. At least have merthiolate and Band-Aids, and preferably roll gauze and tape. A razor blade and snakebite suction cup offer safety for backpackers in rugged country.

Anyone traveling in desert or other remote areas should consider carrying signal flares. Remember, they can be dangerous in the sense that they can start forest fires in dry areas.

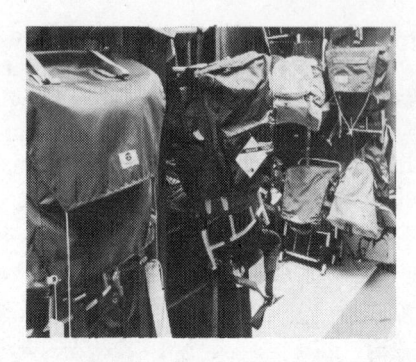

Never purchase a backpack frame without trying it on under full pack, with enough walking to "shake it down." You have to know whether it's going to fit your body size and structure. If it sags, you'll be miserable after a few hours on the trail.

Measuring yourself for a backpack frame depends on the particular frame style. A good backpacker-supply store should have charts to help fit you correctly.

Near home, practice getting into and out of your pack and frame without help. You may not always travel with companions. Find a stump or table you can rest the pack on, about 30 to 36 inches off the ground—about the height of your hips. Balance the pack. Slip your right arm through the right shoulder strap. Pivot and put your left arm through the other. Lean back into the pack. Buckle the front straps, and you're ready to rise.

You should also learn to do this sitting on the ground. Then slide your feet under you and rise to your knees, then up on knee and one foot, and finally stand up. Reverse that procedure to shed your pack in the wilderness: Kneel with your back to a tree. Sit down sideways, and then move your feet out from under you. Unbuckle the front strap. Lean the pack backward and the tree supports the pack upright. Slip your arms free of the shoulder straps.

Rest is important for backpackers and hikers. The experienced backpacker knows when and how to rest. You don't wait until you're absolutely worn out. You manage shorter rests more often.

When you face a long climb, rest at the bottom before you start up, never at the top. Stop, drop your pack, and spread your poncho on the ground. Lie on it and prop your feet up on your pack. Raising your feet up helps anytime you've been walking a lot. Take your shoes off and give them and your feet some air two or three times a day.

When you reach the top of the upgrade and it levels out, keep walking for awhile. You'll relax more efficiently if you don't stop after heavy exertion, but instead proceed with lighter exercise. Applying that principle to hiking, take your rest before you start up the hill. Climb the hill in one major effort and then coast awhile on level ground. Then rest, before the next climb.

But rest. Never let yourself become fatigued. That makes subsequent efforts tougher than they would ordinarily be.

If you're in snake country, you might not want to sleep on the ground. A lightweight string hammock packs easily. All you need is two trees relatively close together.

Not everyone can sleep in a string hammock. It's often because they string it too high off the ground. Hang your hammock about at thigh level. Pull it tight. If it sags much, you'll bend into a horseshoe trying to sleep. You won't need a pillow in your hammock, because your head is already raised considerably.

Hammocks are for sleeping face up, so don't twist yourself into a pretzel trying to sleep another way. Few people can sleep sideways in a hammock without tumbling out.

To get into the hammock, straddle it and sit down. Then lie back, making sure the hammock embraces your shoulders. Finally, lift your feet and place them together in the hammock.

Climbing out is exactly the reverse. Don't go over the side. Lower both feet to the ground, astride the hammock. Stand up and then swing off like you'd get off of a bicycle.

Chapter 11

Relax or Run Ragged?

No one person in the family should become a slave to camping. When you see one person hovering over the cookstove while everyone else sits around doing nothing, you see a group that not only is unfair but doesn't really know how to enjoy a camping vacation.

Don't let your family get bogged down in a rut like this. Camping is best when everyone pitches in for the work and then everyone joins the play. These final pages supply some hints for accomplishing this.

The place to plan participation is at home before you start. Preparing food is a major camp task. Lay out daily menus. Write down exactly what will go into each meal and how much is required.

You gain advantages. First, you have a chance to consider the likes and dislikes of everyone. Pull the whole group into the planning. No one can complain later if meals don't suit them. Second, you save on food costs, because you don't buy more than you really need. Build some flexibility into the menus, because you never know exactly how a day will go or what unexpected activities there will be. Also plan a couple of extra days' meals. Better to bring a little back than not to have enough. (Typically, campers bring back half their food because they've taken too much.)

A third advantage accrues. You can pack in a way that facilitates preparing the meals. It's quicker then to ready your pre-planned meals. This leaves the chief cook more time for relaxation and fun. And after all, that's what the camping is about.

Food preparation takes a lot of time. No one person should have to do it alone. One handy solution revolves around preparing as much as you can of the day's eating in the morning around breakfast time. Peel or wrap potatoes, set out canned vegetables, cut up the salad, and so on. That way you get the worst of the preparation done in the coolest part of the day. You'll plan a light lunch anyway; and then there won't be a long delay while dinner (supper) is being prepared that evening.

At least twice a week, treat the whole family to no-dinner-preparation and no-dinner-dishes. Find a good restaurant somewhere within driving distance of your campsite and go "out" to dinner. It gives a pleasant change from preparing and eating meals at the campsite. Plan these outings into your initial food budget when you do your trip planning. It isn't expensive, when you figure it as part of the cost of camping.

There are many roads to comfort in camping. One takes you to an early-morning swim. It outclasses a shower. It wakes you up, relaxes you, and at the same time invigorates. Unfortunately, most places with a swimming pool don't open it until later, when the day has begun to grow hot. But if you're camping at a lakesite where swimming is permissible and practical, by all means take a dip before breakfast. It'll brighten your whole day.

In hot climates, the natives have a ritual you'd do well to copy on summertime camping jaunts. They call it *siesta*. During the hottest part of the day, after a light lunch, lie down or sit down and be still. After all, you're here to rest and relax—right? Lay out your day so you have no errands to run or chores to do during this hot time. Read or nap. Spray with insect repellant so the flies leave you alone, and just drowse. Siesta is a smooth rejuvenator.

Approach your whole camping philosophy with a comfort-and-relaxation point of view. It leaves the work less unpleasant. After all, the real purpose of camping is to take life easy.